COMPACT HOUSES

The mission of Storey Publishing is to serve our customers by publishing practical information that encourages personal independence in harmony with the environment.

Edited by Nancy Ringer
Art direction by Jessica Armstrong
Book design by MacFadden and Thorpe
Illustrations by Steve Sanford
Plan drawings by the author, edited by Ilona Sherratt
Indexed by Catherine F. Goddard

Storey books are available for special premium and promotional uses and for customized editions. For further information, please call 1-800-793-9396.

Storey Publishing
210 MASS MoCA Way
North Adams, MA 01247
www.storey.com

Printed in the United States by CJK
10 9 8 7 6 5 4 3 2 1

LIBRARY OF CONGRESS CATALOGING-IN-PUBLICATION DATA

Rowan, Gerald.
 Compact houses / By Gerald Rowan.
   pages cm
 Includes index.
 ISBN 978-1-61212-102-4 (pbk. : alk. paper)
 ISBN 978-1-60342-861-3 (ebook)
 1. Small houses. I. Title.
TH4890.R69 2013
728'.37—dc23
                    2013012524

Storey Publishing is committed to making environmentally responsible manufacturing decisions. This book was printed on paper made from sustainably harvested fiber.

COMPACT HOUSES

50 CREATIVE FLOOR PLANS FOR EFFICIENT, WELL-DESIGNED SMALL HOMES

by Gerald Rowan

Illustrations by Steve Sanford

Storey Publishing

INTRODUCTION:
WHY LIVE SMALL?

MOST OF US DREAM OF HAVING A PLACE OF OUR OWN. SOME OF US DREAM LARGE, BUT MORE AND MORE OF US ARE DREAMING OF SOMETHING SMALL.

Perhaps we long to own our first house — something on the smaller side because we're just starting out. Perhaps we are empty nesters, downsizing into more practical space. Perhaps we want to build a little place of our own, with our own hands. Perhaps we want to build small in order to live mortgage-free. Perhaps we want to minimize the impact of our home on the environment.

Whatever the reason, a compact home offers advantages across the board: reduced building time, reduced use of building materials, less impact on the environment, smaller carbon footprint, and less maintenance once it's built. With these savings, a compact home also allows for quality materials, solid craftsmanship, and even a few touches of luxury. These characteristics would appeal to any homeowner.

Some potential homeowners may object to the idea of a small house, perhaps equating the concept of *small* with cramped, crowded living quarters. But with good design, a compact home is a comfortable one. It feels welcoming. As with any home, its particular character depends on its designers and owners. Some may want their compact home to be warm and cozy; others may prefer a more spartan aesthetic, with neatness and efficiency the ruling principles. The point is that design, not square footage, determines a home's worthiness. And good design is the focus of this book.

This book is intended for folks who want to have a hand in designing or building a compact home that fits their needs in a simple, affordable, ecologically sustainable way. Whether you are a home designer, builder, owner, or some combination of the three, you'll find useful advice here on the criteria for

Engineering and Codes

Though this book offers many design ideas and plans, if you are not a builder or architect, you will need to work with one, or a construction engineer, to create a detailed building plan. You will also need to consult with your local government's building department to make sure that your plans conform to local building and zoning codes.

critical house elements, such as room layouts, power sources, appliances, furnishings, and space-saving (or space-enhancing) design features. Each element plays a role in the aesthetic and functioning of the home, but most important is the way in which all the elements work together. Successful small-space design is a gestalt process. *Gestalt* describes a group of components that function as a unit and are so integrated that the unit's properties are not derivable by a summation of the components. In other words, the whole is more than the sum of its parts. That's the beauty of a well-designed compact home.

In this book you'll find dozens of original home designs in a range of styles and a variety of sizes, from around 800 to 1,400 square feet. But this book is not just for those looking to build a new home. There is a vast range of compact homes already in existence, from bungalows and ranches to Capes and condominiums. Many are in dire need of renovation and thus are available cheap. With a little forethought and consideration of the design imperatives for small-space living, you can readily transform these houses into comfortable, efficient, stylish homes. You can convert a cookie-cutter Cape into a quirky, modern abode; retrofit a dark, dingy ranch into a sleek, open-plan "green" dwelling; or renovate a shabby old farmhouse to make it the warm, welcoming home it was meant to be.

All advice notwithstanding, I hope to encourage you to draw on your own creativity, building on the concepts developed in this book to arrive at a home plan that is both personal and well designed. Our home is a part of our identity. It is our launching pad and our refuge. To truly serve us well, it must clearly reflect our lifestyle and values. That makes it important to choose the design ideas that are best for *us*. We are all anxious to jump into our house project, get our hands dirty, and move in as soon as possible. The time we spend up front in the design phase will pay off in a number of ways, reducing building time, helping us avoid mistakes, and adding to our long-term satisfaction.

CHAPTER 1

PLANS: 50 DESIGNS FOR COMPACT HOUSES

THE 50 DESIGNS IN THIS CHAPTER ARE MEANT TO SERVE AS A STARTING POINT FOR FOLKS WHO WANT TO HAVE A HAND IN DESIGNING THEIR OWN SPACE.

The designs are not intended to be final plans. Even if you fall in love with one particular design shown here, you'll want to tweak it to make it work for your site, living needs, and aesthetic, and you should work with a builder, architect, or construction engineer to arrive at a working building plan.

The designs are roughly organized first by the number of floors (single-story homes followed by two-story ones) and then the square footage, from smaller to larger. Each design notes the square footage of the home, the number of bedrooms, the number and size of bathrooms, and any unique features, such as a fireplace or an open living plan. Feel free to mix and match elements, incorporating those you like into whatever turns out to be your dream-home design. Kitchens and bathrooms are particularly interchangeable. And don't feel limited to using these designs just for new homes; many of the ideas suggested here can be incorporated into existing houses (see chapter 4 for more on that topic).

Each floor plan is accompanied by an outside view of the home, an illustration showing *one* style in which the home could be built. Keep in mind that these drawings are just ideas. Any floor plan can be executed in numerous styles, with any number of siding materials and roofing options. What you see here is an interpretation of the floor plan, not a mandate. This is *your* house, and it should suit *your* style and needs.

The designs are named for sites and natural places in my home state of Pennsylvania. Many were inspired by those specific locations — a home with a 270-degree view named for a hilltop, for example, or a home designed for a wooded setting named for a state forest. You can call them whatever you like, of course.

Note: These floor plans are meant to serve as design inspirations, not decrees. They can — and should — be changed to suit individual aesthetics and needs, along with the peculiar demands and limitations of the specific building site. Though each of the plans lists its interior square footage, this is an approximate measurement. Any changes you make to the plans will, of course, change the dimensions and square footages. Even if against all odds you decide to follow a plan exactly, your builder's construction decisions — using 2×6 versus 2×4 framing, for example — will affect the exact square footage. Here again, I can't emphasize enough the importance of working with a reputable, experienced builder, architect, or construction engineer.

Bathroom Definitions

A *full* bathroom contains a tub, a toilet, and a sink. A *three-quarter* bathroom contains a shower, a toilet, and a sink. A *half* bathroom contains just a toilet and a sink. A *Japanese-style bathroom* is one in which the bathtub, toilet, and sink are each in their own space, with a door or screen separating them from one another (see page 128 for more on Japanese-style bathrooms). A *rain shower* is a specialty shower head that uses gravity to release large drops of water. Gentle, yet still effective.

ABBREVIATIONS

BB = bunk bed

C = upholstered chair

CR = crib

CT = coffee table

D = dresser

DT = dining table

E = entertainment center

ET = end table (or side table)

FB = full-size bed

HW = hot water heater

NS = nightstand

S = sofa

R = refrigerator

SB = sideboard (or buffet)

SH = shelving (or storage cabinet)

TB = twin bed

Key to Furniture Arrangements

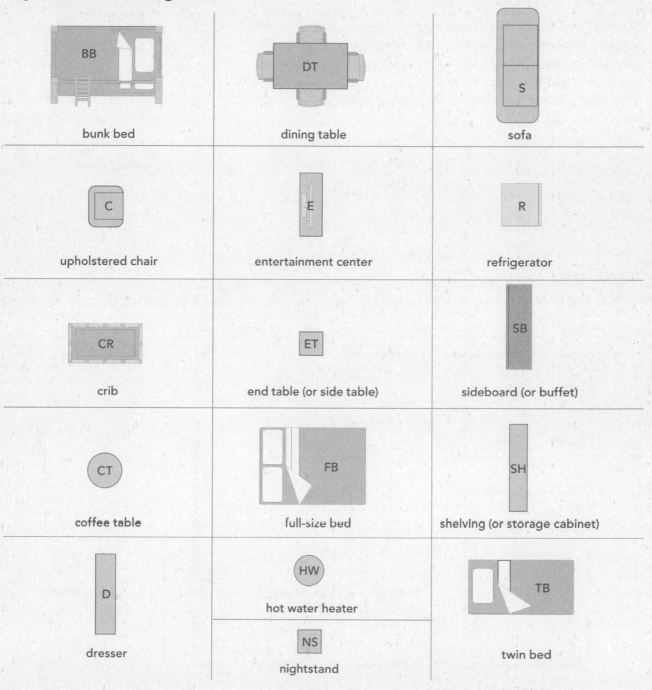

bunk bed

dining table

sofa

upholstered chair

entertainment center

refrigerator

crib

end table (or side table)

sideboard (or buffet)

coffee table

full-size bed

shelving (or storage cabinet)

dresser

hot water heater

twin bed

nightstand

FIRST FORK

A super-compact design with great potential for energy efficiency, bundled into a home with a modern aesthetic and stylish details. The open-concept living space is easy to heat with a fuel-burning stove, and operable clerestory windows allow for natural ventilation in warmer weather. For a similar but slightly larger layout, see Cook Forest (page 16).

Features

814 square feet

2 bedrooms

1 full bathroom

Open-concept living space

Fuel-burning stove

Multiple decks

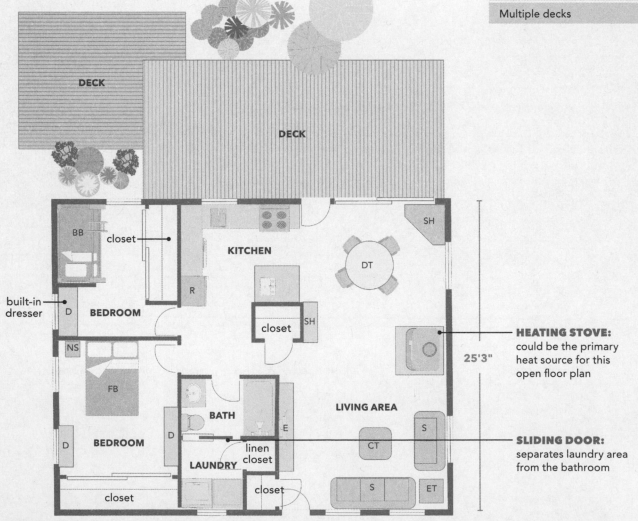

DECK

DECK

BB

closet

built-in dresser

D   BEDROOM

NS

FB

D   BEDROOM

closet

KITCHEN

R

closet   SH

BATH

D

LAUNDRY

linen closet

closet

SH

DT

E

LIVING AREA

CT   S

S   ET

25'3"

32'3"

HEATING STOVE: could be the primary heat source for this open floor plan

SLIDING DOOR: separates laundry area from the bathroom

PITCHED ROOF: could support solar panels if oriented to the south

CLERESTORY WINDOWS: bring light to the interior and can be opened in warm weather for natural ventilation

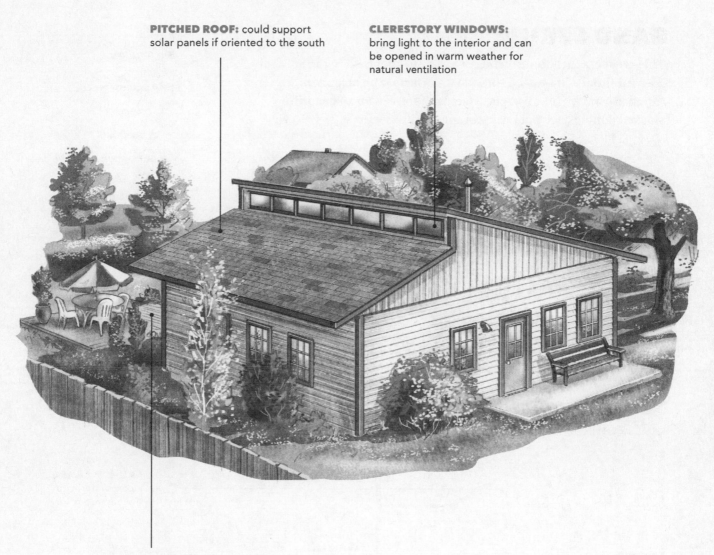

DOUBLE DECKS: a nice setup for a family that enjoys being outside; you could easily add a hot tub or water feature to either deck

SAND SPRING

This very compact home blends privacy and openness to the outdoors, with minimal windows on the side walls facing the neighbors, an expansive but high wall of glass facing the street, and a beautiful stacked double deck out back, complete with hot tub.

Features

884 square feet

2 bedrooms

1 full bathroom

Open-concept kitchen/living space

Fuel-burning stove

Multiple decks

HEATING STOVE:
could be the primary heat source for this open floor plan

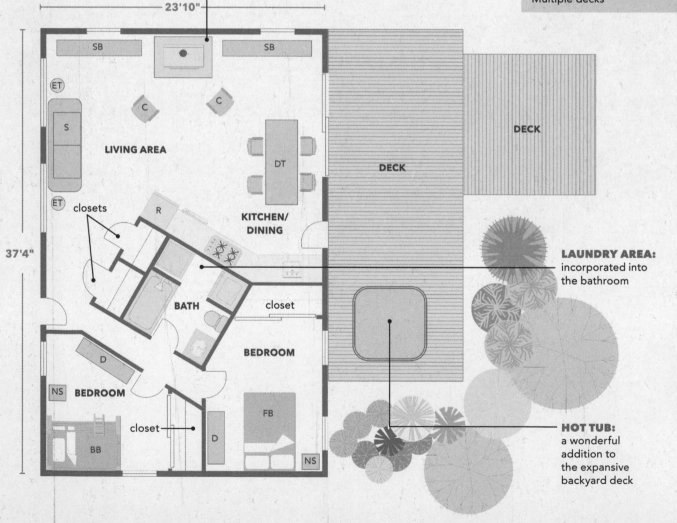

23'10"

37'4"

SB

SB

ET

C

S

C

LIVING AREA

DT

ET

closets

R

KITCHEN/ DINING

DECK

DECK

BATH

closet

LAUNDRY AREA:
incorporated into the bathroom

BEDROOM

D

NS

BEDROOM

closet

D

BB

FB

NS

HOT TUB:
a wonderful addition to the expansive backyard deck

HIGH WALL OF WINDOWS: bring light and a sense of space to the interior, without impinging upon privacy

STEEP ROOF: allows for a high ceiling and a general sense of spaciousness indoors

DOUBLE DECKS: create an inviting outdoor living space

COOK FOREST

This design, similar to First Fork (page 12) sets the bedrooms and bathrooms in a private wing. The rest of the house is an open-concept living space, with the kitchen and dining area integrated with the living area. Skylights and clerestory windows bring light into the core of the house.

Features

912 square feet

2 bedrooms

1 full bathroom

Open-concept living area

Fireplace

Multiple decks

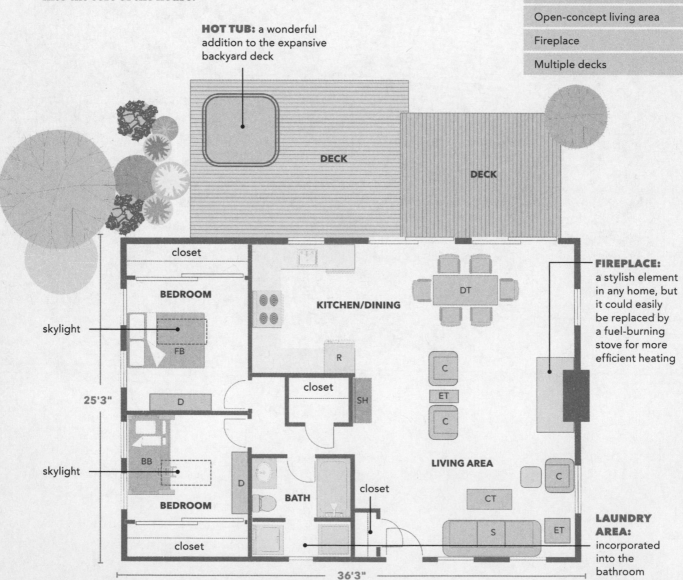

HOT TUB: a wonderful addition to the expansive backyard deck

FIREPLACE: a stylish element in any home, but it could easily be replaced by a fuel-burning stove for more efficient heating

LAUNDRY AREA: incorporated into the bathroom

skylight

skylight

25'3"

36'3"

DECK

DECK

closet

BEDROOM

FB

D

BB

BEDROOM

closet

KITCHEN/DINING

R

closet

SH

D

BATH

closet

DT

C

ET

C

LIVING AREA

C

CT

S

ET

CLERESTORY WINDOWS: bring light to the main living area and can be opened in warm weather for natural ventilation

PITCHED ROOF: could support solar panels if oriented to the south

SKYLIGHTS: offer a view to the sky from the bedrooms

DEEP ROOF OVERHANG: shades the windows during the summer months, helping to keep the house cool

CHERRY SPRINGS

Both the sunroom and the fireplace area can be isolated from the rest of the home with glass sliding doors, cutting down the floorspace that must be heated in colder weather. This is an ideal home for a young couple just starting out; it can easily be added on to later.

Features

940 square feet

1 bedroom

1 full bathroom

Kitchen island

Fireplace

Sunroom

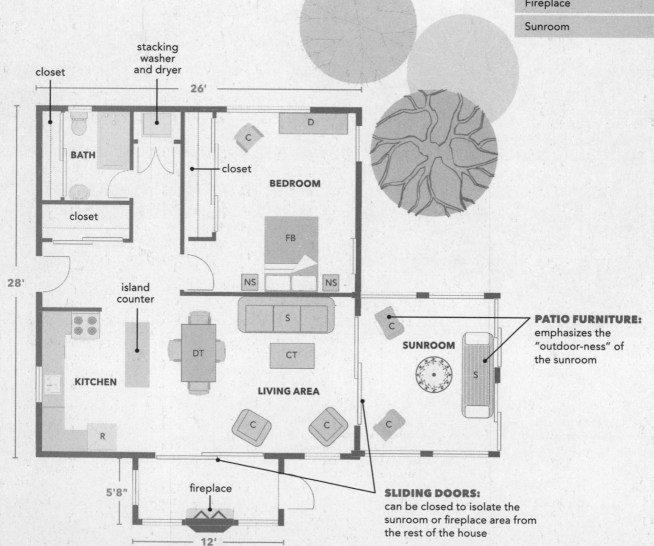

closet

stacking washer and dryer

26'

BATH

closet

closet

BEDROOM

C

D

FB

NS   NS

28'

island counter

S

KITCHEN

DT

CT

LIVING AREA

R

C   C

C

SUNROOM

C

S

PATIO FURNITURE: emphasizes the "outdoor-ness" of the sunroom

5'8"

fireplace

12'

SLIDING DOORS: can be closed to isolate the sunroom or fireplace area from the rest of the house

SOLAR PANELS: bring a welcome measure of energy independence to the home

HIGH WALL OF WINDOWS: helps the sunroom feel open to the outdoors from top to bottom

BIG SPRING

This is a great house for raising kids. The sliding door between the two back bedrooms allows the space to be converted into a large playroom, perfect for days when it's cold and wet outside. The open concept maximizes the usable space for a growing family.

Features

961 square feet

3 bedrooms

1 full bathroom

Open-concept living area

Fuel-burning stove

Multiple decks

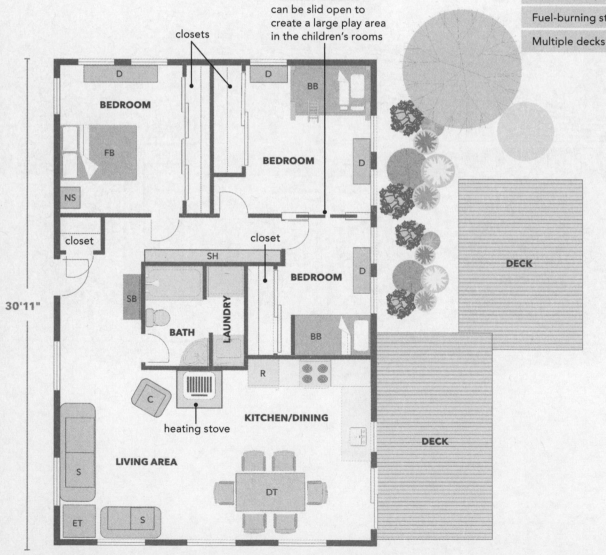

POCKET DOORS: can be slid open to create a large play area in the children's rooms

closets

closet

closet

BEDROOM

FB

NS

D   D   BB

BEDROOM

D

SH

SB

BATH   LAUNDRY   BEDROOM   D

C   BB

heating stove   R

KITCHEN/DINING

DECK

DECK

LIVING AREA

S

ET   S   DT

30'11"

25'4"

BEDROOMS: are cozily tucked under the lower roofline

ANGLED ROOFLINE: allows for a cathedral ceiling over the main living space

DOUBLE DECKS: create an inviting outdoor living space

SAW MILL CREEK

This modern design has a double-pitched roof, angling in from opposite sides; a water catchment system installed here could easily provide for all the landscaping's irrigation needs. A deep closet adjacent to the bathroom can hold the mechanical systems (hot water heater, furnace, and so on), allowing you to build this home on a concrete slab, rather than a full-depth foundation; this can save money and expands your siting options.

Features
988 square feet
2 bedrooms
1 full bathroom
Open-concept living space
Kitchen island
Fuel-burning stove
Deck

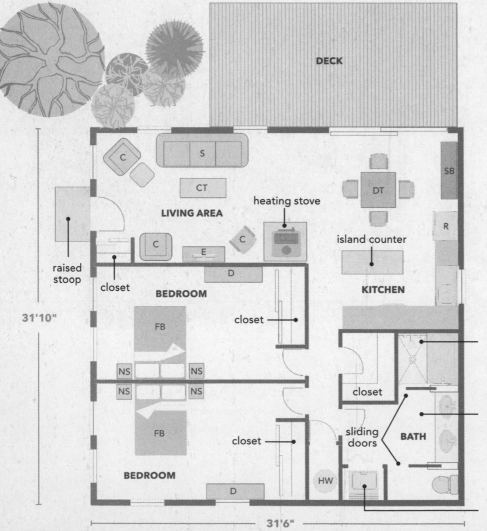

DECK

C

S

CT

LIVING AREA

heating stove

SB

DT

island counter

R

C

C

E

D

raised stoop

closet

BEDROOM

KITCHEN

closet

FB

NS   NS

NS   NS

closet

31'10"

FB

closet

sliding doors

BATH

HW

BEDROOM

D

31'6"

RAIN SHOWER: a luxurious open unit adjacent to the tub

JAPANESE-STYLE BATHROOM: a flexible design that allows privacy for multiple users

stacking washer and dryer

WATER CATCHMENT SYSTEM: can be installed in the backyard where the two angled rooflines meet

CLERESTORY WINDOWS: bring light to the interior and can be opened in warm weather for natural ventilation

WHITE HAVEN

This long, narrow design lends itself well to modular construction; it can be built off-site and trucked in. With its front wall given a southern orientation, it becomes a passive solar home. The windowless back wall can be built into a hillside for its insulative and protective capacity.

Features

1,000 square feet
2 bedrooms
1 full bathroom
Open-concept living space
Woodstove or fireplace
Deck
Passive solar applications

RAIN SHOWER: a luxurious open unit adjacent to the tub

GLASS BLOCK WALLS: allow light into the interior rooms

HOT WATER HEATER: can be set, with other mechanicals, in the back of this deep closet, precluding the need for a basement

closet

sliding door

changing table

closet

63'

16'4"

closet

Fireplace or heating stove

BEDROOM

LAUNDRY

BATH

BEDROOM

KITCHEN

LIVING AREA

DECK

ARBOR: can be planted with vines or trellising plants to provide shade during the summer

BACK WALL: is designed to be set into a hillside or to the north, providing insulative protection

LONG WALL OF GLASS DOORS AND WINDOWS: is designed to be oriented to the south for passive solar applications

ALLEGHENY FRONT

With its flat roof, this house is designed for a warm climate.
Operable clerestory windows encircle the house, shielded by a
deep roof overhang, providing for plentiful natural ventilation
even in wet weather.

Features

1,011 square feet

2 bedrooms

1 full bathroom

Open-concept living space

Kitchen peninsula

Fuel-burning stove

Deck

**JAPANESE-STYLE
BATHROOM:** a flexible
design that allows privacy
for multiple users

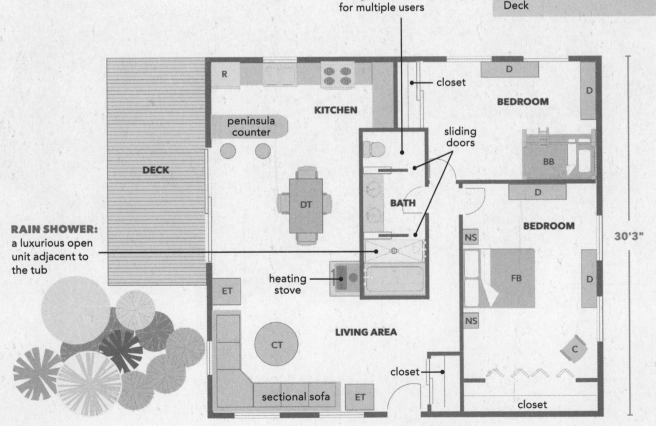

closet

sliding
doors

RAIN SHOWER:
a luxurious open
unit adjacent to
the tub

heating
stove

closet

closet

KITCHEN

peninsula
counter

DECK

DT

BATH

BEDROOM

BB

D

D

D

D

BEDROOM

NS

FB

D

NS

C

ET

CT

LIVING AREA

sectional sofa

ET

R

30'3"

33'5"

DEEP ROOF OVERHANG:
shades the windows and protects
them against rain, helping to keep
the house cool

CLERESTORY WINDOWS:
encircle the perimeter of the home
and combine with the flat roof to
give the home a modern look

ROCK PASS

This is a wonderful design for warmer climates, with natural ventilation provided by sliding glass doors surrounding the central garden. With the open side of the house oriented southward, passive solar heating keeps the house warm during the colder months.

Features

1,014 square feet

2 bedrooms

1 full bathroom

Fireplace

Pantry

Semi-enclosed courtyard

Passive solar applications

FLOOR-TO-CEILING CABINETS: provide ample pantry storage right in the kitchen area

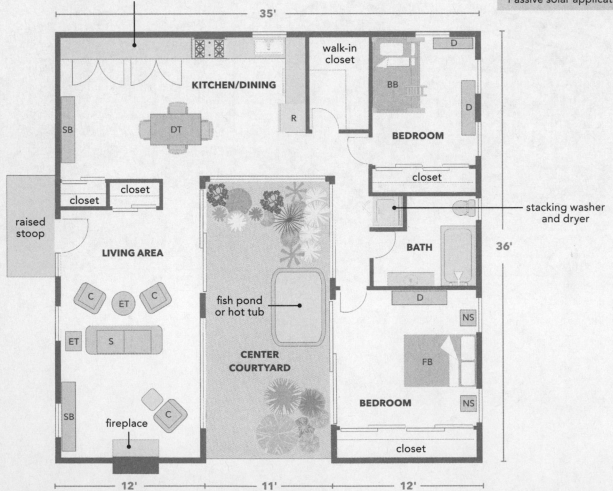

GLASS PANELS AND DOORS: allow for passive solar heating and natural ventilation.

CENTER COURTYARD: a private retreat for relaxing, bathing, gardening, and other endeavors

CANOE CREEK

This open-concept home has clerestory windows on three sides and a cathedral ceiling over the main living space, making the interior feel quite bright and roomy. When oriented with the sunroom facing south, it has possible passive solar applications.

Features

1,039 square feet
2 bedrooms
1 full bathroom
Kitchen peninsula
Fuel-burning stove
Sunroom with skylights
Deck
Covered porch

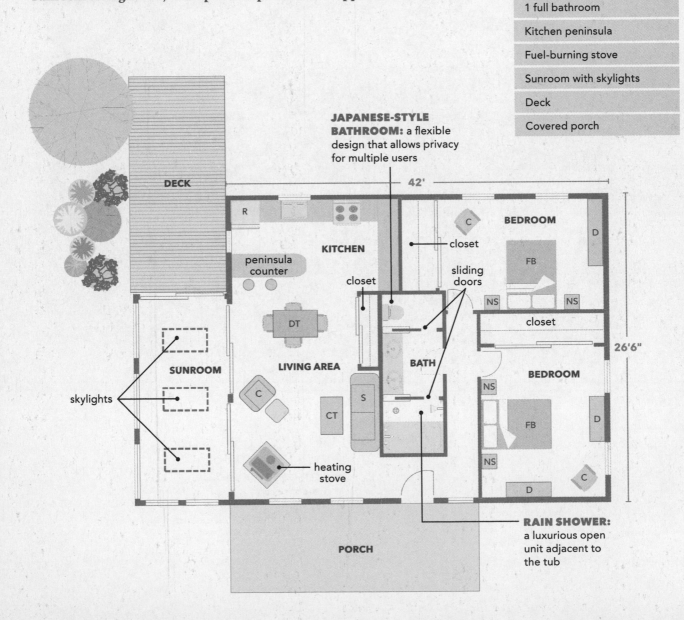

JAPANESE-STYLE BATHROOM: a flexible design that allows privacy for multiple users

DECK

42'

R

KITCHEN

closet

BEDROOM

C

closet

D

FB

peninsula counter

sliding doors

NS

NS

closet

26'6"

DT

BATH

skylights

SUNROOM

LIVING AREA

BEDROOM

C

NS

FB

D

S

CT

NS

heating stove

C

D

RAIN SHOWER: a luxurious open unit adjacent to the tub

PORCH

CLERESTORY WINDOWS:
bring light to the interior and can
be opened in warm weather for
natural ventilation

LONG SLOPED ROOF:
allows for a cathedral ceiling
over the main living space

SUNROOM: a bright space
with skylights and open views
in three directions

RUXTON

Sliding panels throughout this home allow for flexible living arrangements. The dining space can be separated from the living space by a shoji screen, and the garden atrium can be accessed from any side by the sliding glass doors. The atrium functions as a central light well, allowing sunlight to penetrate the core of the building.

Features

1,056 square feet	
2 bedrooms	
1 full bathroom	
Fireplace	
Atrium	
Deck	

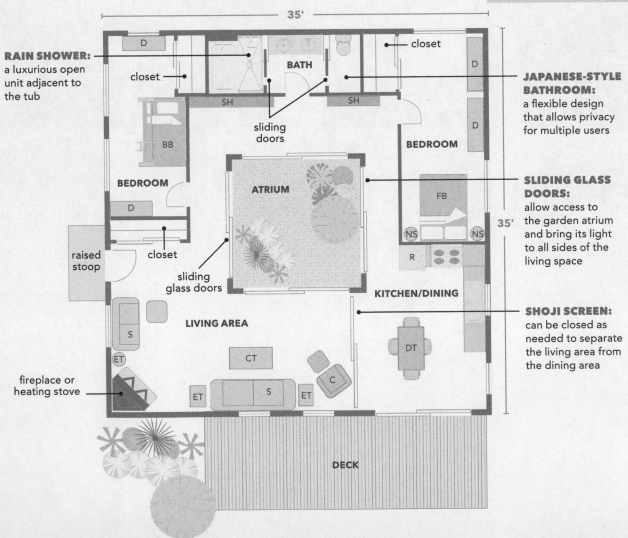

RAIN SHOWER: a luxurious open unit adjacent to the tub

JAPANESE-STYLE BATHROOM: a flexible design that allows privacy for multiple users

SLIDING GLASS DOORS: allow access to the garden atrium and bring its light to all sides of the living space

SHOJI SCREEN: can be closed as needed to separate the living area from the dining area

fireplace or heating stove

35'

35'

closet

BATH

closet

sliding doors

closet

BB

BEDROOM

D

raised stoop

closet

sliding glass doors

ATRIUM

BEDROOM

FB

NS   NS

R

KITCHEN/DINING

DT

LIVING AREA

CT

C

S

ET

S   ET

ET

DECK

LIGHT WELL: formed by glass panels at the peak of the roof brings natural light to the atrium garden

SQUARE DESIGN: works with the central atrium to give the home a unique interior space

SLIDING GLASS DOORS: offer an expansive view of the outdoors from the kitchen and dining area

PINE RIDGE

This bright and comfortable home offers both a garage and a sunporch. The fireplace in the living room corner can be designed as an eye-catching focal point, with a fieldstone chimney and adjacent masonry seats, or as a more petite woodstove, with an unobtrusive stovepipe chimney.

Features

1,100 square feet

2 bedrooms

1 full bathroom

Kitchen peninsula

Fireplace

Fuel-burning stove

Sunroom

Garage

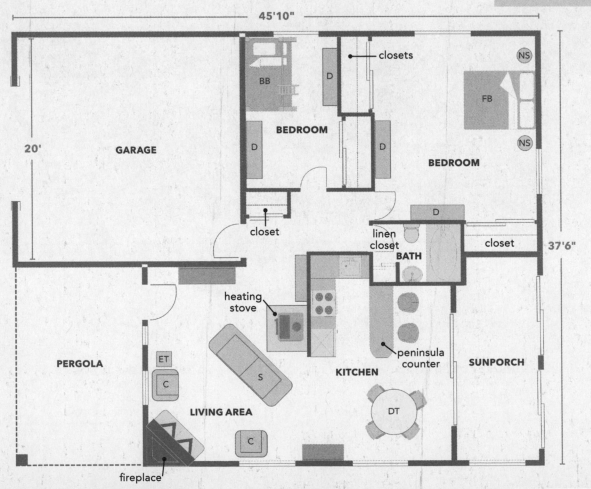

CLERESTORY WINDOWS: bring light to the interior and can be opened in warm weather for natural ventilation

INTEGRATED GARAGE: is a classic element in suburban architecture, providing convenient sheltered passage from car to home

PERGOLA: defines the span of the entry; it could easily be converted to a solid roof for a covered porch

BUFFALO CREEK

This design is set up to use solar panels on its roof; if you replaced these panels with skylights, the home could also have passive solar applications. The master bedroom affords a great deal of privacy.

Features

1,136 square feet

3 bedrooms

1 full and 1 three-quarter bathroom

Fireplace

Deck

Photovoltaic array

Passive solar applications

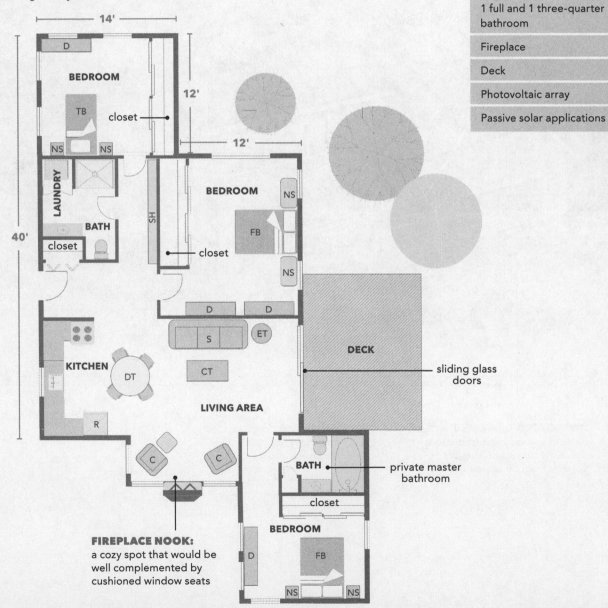

14'

12'

12'

40'

BEDROOM

TB

closet

NS   NS

LAUNDRY

BATH

closet

SH

BEDROOM

NS

FB

NS

closet

D   D

S   ET

CT

KITCHEN

DT

R

C   C

LIVING AREA

DECK

sliding glass doors

BATH

private master bathroom

closet

FIREPLACE NOOK: a cozy spot that would be well complemented by cushioned window seats

BEDROOM

D

FB

NS   NS

ROOFLINE: is designed to accommodate solar panels and should be oriented to the south

MASTER BEDROOM: is set in its own private "wing," making this an ideal plan for growing families

ROOF OVERHANG: could be extended to accommodate additional solar panels

ROTHROCK

With a deck and a patio, this open-concept one-level house lends itself to outdoor living. It has the potential to be a very energy-efficient design, particularly if the fireplace is replaced with a woodstove.

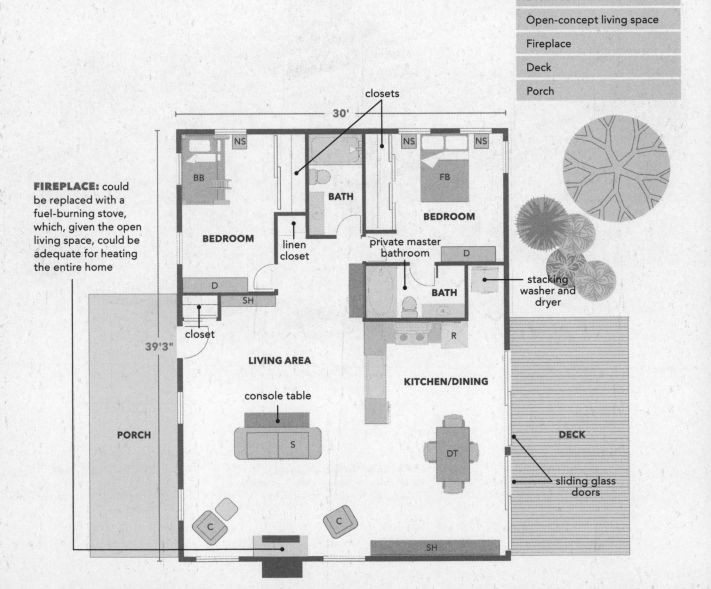

closets

30'

NS

BB

FIREPLACE: could be replaced with a fuel-burning stove, which, given the open living space, could be adequate for heating the entire home

BATH

NS   FB   NS

BEDROOM

BEDROOM

linen closet

private master bathroom

D

stacking washer and dryer

39'3"

D

SH

closet

BATH

R

LIVING AREA

KITCHEN/DINING

console table

PORCH

S

DECK

DT

C   C

SH

sliding glass doors

FLAT ROOF: gives the home a contemporary look but is best suited for regions with little precipitation

FRONT PORCH: a nice spot for relaxing on a warm day and shelter for visitors waiting at the door

BOARD-AND-BATTEN SIDING: is a good choice for a modern design in a rustic setting, blending the clean lines of contemporary style with a cottage aesthetic

OXBOW BEND

If oriented southward, the glass "light well" bump-out in the dining area allows light to flood into this house. This feature makes this home appropriate for a wooded lot, allowing maximum light into the structure while at the same time providing an expansive view of the outdoors.

Features

1,176 square feet

2 bedrooms

1 full bathroom

Open-concept living space

Solar atrium

Fireplace

LIGHT WELL:
opens up the interior to the outside, bringing natural light and an expansive view

26'4"

SB

fireplace

C

LIVING AREA

S

DT

CT

DINING

S

sliding glass doors

console table

peninsula counter

KITCHEN

40'

closet

PORCH

ENTRY WITH CLOSET:
provides ample space for storing coats, shoes, and outdoor gear

ENTRY

D

closets

R

D

BEDROOM

NS

BEDROOM

SH

FB

stacking washer and dryer

FB

NS

NS

BATH

closet

12'

skylight

RAIN SHOWER:
a luxurious open unit adjacent to the tub

MASONRY FIREPLACE: can efficiently heat the entirety of this open-concept home

SKYLIGHT: provides natural light and ventilation in the bathroom

COVERED PORCH: shelters visitors to the home from inclement weather

CALDONIA

This home wraps itself around an outdoor courtyard that could accommodate a garden, lap pool, or fish pond. The sliding glass doors on all sides of the courtyard provide excellent summer ventilation, and if the open side of that outdoor living space were oriented southward, the home could take advantage of passive solar heating.

Features

| **1,190 square feet** |
| Open-concept living space |
| Large storage cabinets |
| Fireplace |
| Semi-enclosed courtyard |
| Passive solar applications |

2 bedrooms

1 full bathroom

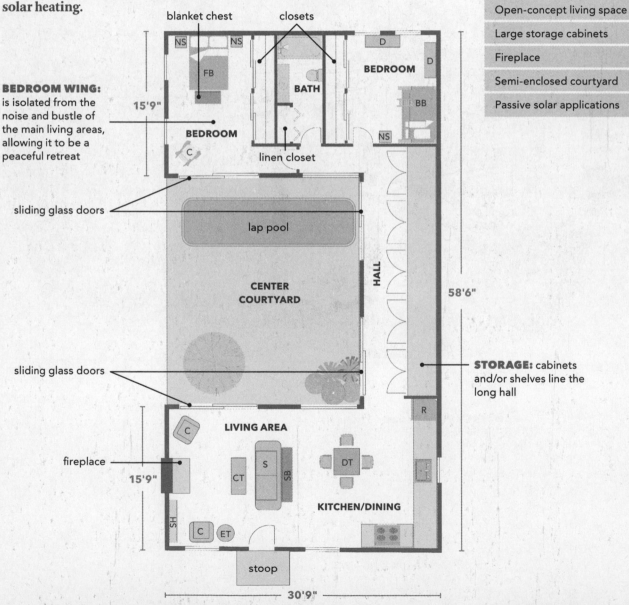

blanket chest

closets

BEDROOM WING: is isolated from the noise and bustle of the main living areas, allowing it to be a peaceful retreat

15'9"

BEDROOM

BATH

BEDROOM

linen closet

sliding glass doors

lap pool

CENTER COURTYARD

HALL

58'6"

sliding glass doors

STORAGE: cabinets and/or shelves line the long hall

fireplace

LIVING AREA

15'9"

KITCHEN/DINING

stoop

30'9"

CLERESTORY WINDOWS: frame two sides of each wing, imbuing the house with a wealth of natural light

CENTER COURTYARD: can be designed to suit the needs of the homeowners, with anything from a lap pool to a vegetable garden to a Zen-style meditation spot

SLIDING GLASS DOORS: on opposite sides of the courtyard provide excellent cross-ventilation, making it easy to keep this house comfortable in warm weather

BALD EAGLE

The sunroom adds living space and the potential for passive solar heating. With bedrooms in separate "wings" and two bathrooms, this is an ideal design for a growing family.

Features

1,277 square feet

3 bedrooms

2 full bathrooms

Open-concept living space

Sunroom with skylights

Deck

Passive solar applications

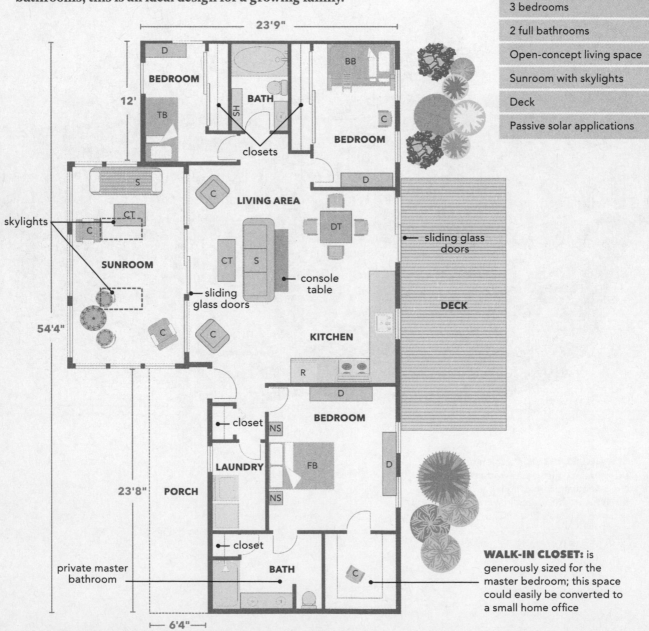

skylights

sliding glass doors

console table

sliding glass doors

private master bathroom

WALK-IN CLOSET: is generously sized for the master bedroom; this space could easily be converted to a small home office

PITCHED ROOF: could support solar panels if oriented to the south

BEDROOM WINGS: separate the children's bedrooms from the parents', making this an ideal plan for a family

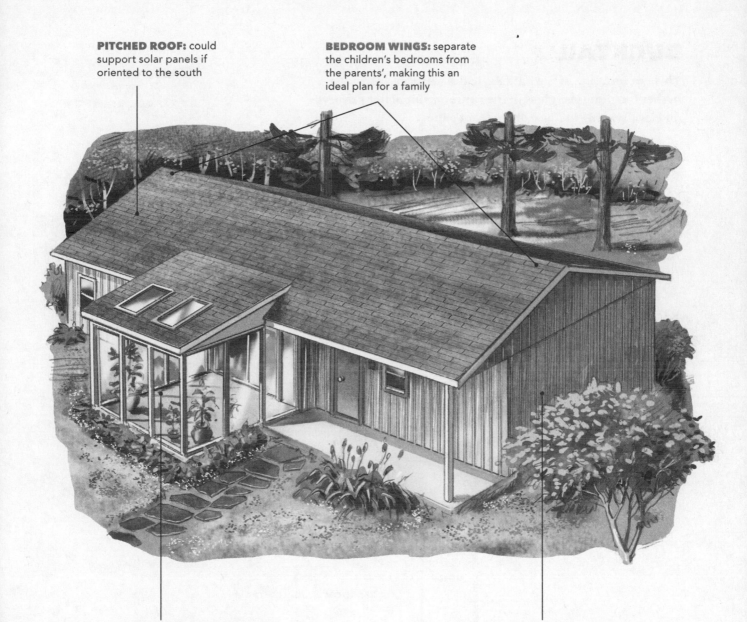

SUNROOM: is open to the outdoors from floor to ceiling; it can be oriented to the south for passive solar heating

WINDOW-LESS END WALL: is designed for privacy from adjacent lots; in a more secluded spot, windows could be added

BUCKTAIL

This is a variation of the Bald Eagle design (page 44), with a
higher roof line, less glass in the sunroom (for better privacy),
and landscaping in place of the front patio.

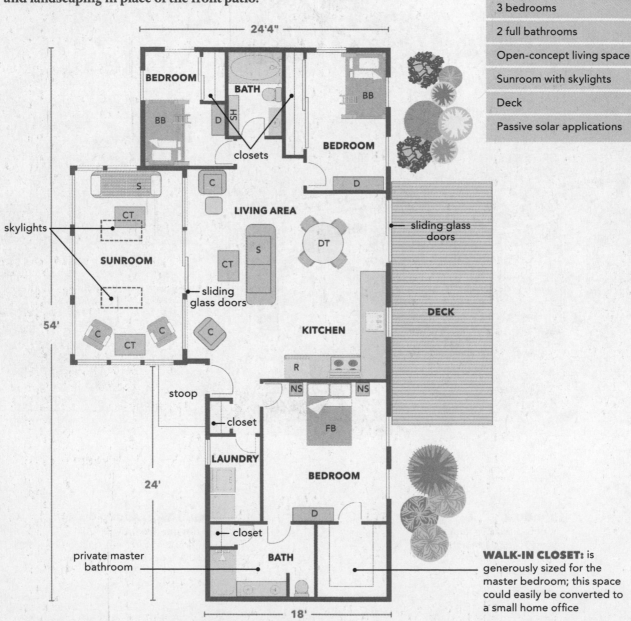

skylights

SUNROOM

54'

24'

private master
bathroom

stoop

closet

LAUNDRY

closet

BATH

18'

24'4"

BEDROOM

BB

BATH

D SH

closets

C

CT

SUNROOM

C C

CT C

sliding
glass doors

S

CT

S

LIVING AREA

DT

KITCHEN

R

NS NS

FB

BEDROOM

D

BB

BEDROOM

D

sliding glass
doors

DECK

WALK-IN CLOSET: is
generously sized for the
master bedroom; this space
could easily be converted to
a small home office

Features

1,277 square feet

3 bedrooms

2 full bathrooms

Open-concept living space

Sunroom with skylights

Deck

Passive solar applications

PITCHED ROOF: could support solar panels if oriented to the south

BEDROOM WINGS: separate the children's bedrooms from the parents', making this an ideal plan for a family

HIGH ROOFLINE: allows for a cathedral ceiling over the main living space

CLERESTORY WINDOWS: bring light to the interior and can be opened in warm weather for natural ventilation

BLUE KNOB

Unlike many compact home designs, this design offers a spacious living room separate from the noise and bustle of the kitchen. Either of the bedrooms could be adapted for use as a home office.

Features

1,280 square feet
2 bedrooms
2 full and 1 half bathrooms
Pantry
Fireplace
Deck

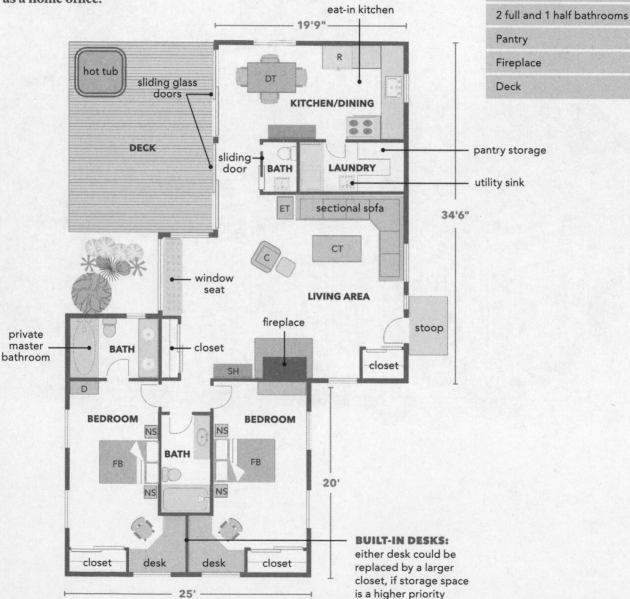

eat-in kitchen

19'9"

hot tub

sliding glass doors

DT

R

KITCHEN/DINING

DECK

sliding door

BATH

LAUNDRY

pantry storage

utility sink

34'6"

ET

sectional sofa

C

CT

window seat

LIVING AREA

fireplace

stoop

private master bathroom

BATH

closet

SH

closet

D

BEDROOM

NS

NS

BEDROOM

FB

BATH

FB

NS

NS

closet

desk

desk

closet

25'

20'

BUILT-IN DESKS: either desk could be replaced by a larger closet, if storage space is a higher priority

HOT TUB: is optional for any home design; this would also be a nice spot for a water garden

BEDROOM WING: shelters the sleeping quarters from the main living space

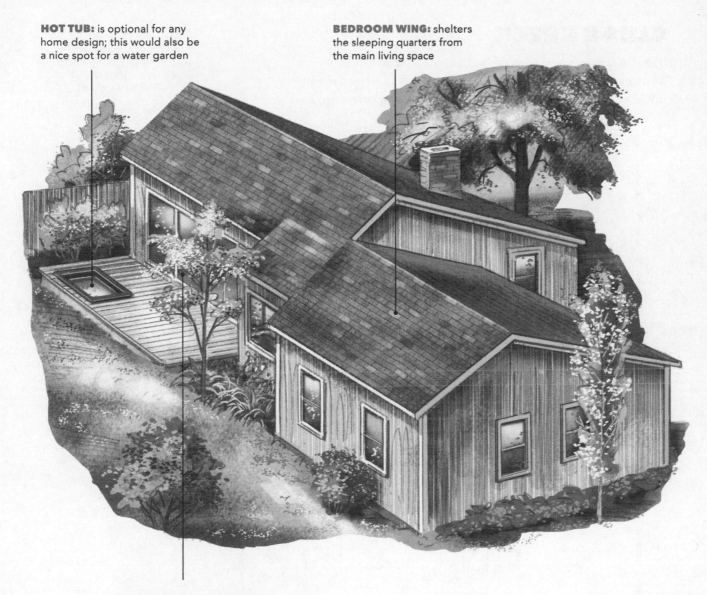

DOUBLED SETS OF SLIDING GLASS DOORS: flood the dining, kitchen, and living areas with natural light and provide a great view of the backyard

CLEAR CREEK

This home features spacious bedrooms, including a master bedroom suite. It's designed to be built atop a full basement, with stairs in the kitchen leading down. Built-in storage in the living room conceals an entertainment center.

Features

1,310 square feet

3 bedrooms

2 full bathrooms

Deck

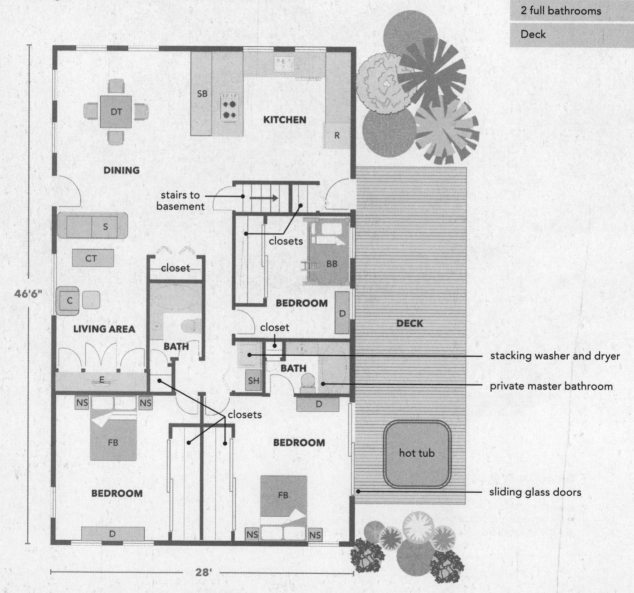

HIGH LOUVERED VENTS:
can be used for ventilation or
replaced with decorative windows

EXPANSIVE BACKYARD DECK:
can easily accommodate a hot tub
or container garden

BRIAR RIDGE

This unusual modern design features a very private master bedroom, with the kids' bedrooms at the opposite end of the house. This is an excellent passive solar design and can be situated to take advantage of a spectactular view.

Features

1,366 square feet

3 bedrooms

2 full bathrooms

Open-concept living space

Passive solar applications

Deck

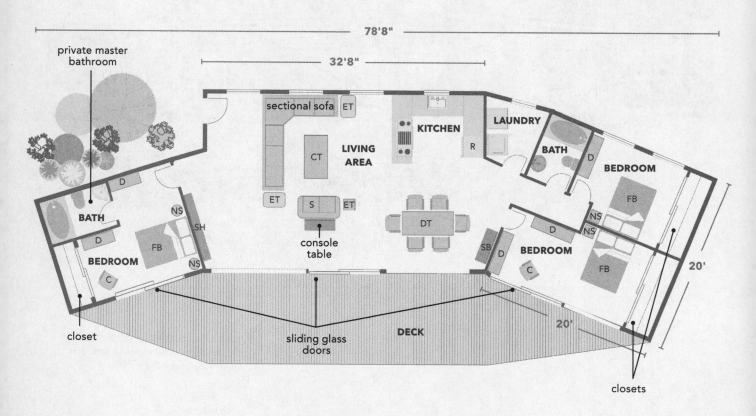

private master bathroom

78'8"

32'8"

sectional sofa   ET

KITCHEN

LAUNDRY

LIVING AREA

CT

R

BATH

BEDROOM

D

FB

BATH

D   ET

NS

SH

ET   S   ET

FB   NS

NS

console table

DT

D

BEDROOM

FB

BEDROOM

SB   D

C

closet

C

20'

sliding glass doors

DECK

20'

closets

SEMICIRCULAR LAYOUT: is perfect for capturing a great view; this home would work well on a waterfront or mountaintop

SLIDING GLASS DOORS: provide access to the outdoors from any section of the home, as well as light and ventilation

WIDE DECK: visually ties together the two ends of the house and eases the transition from indoors to out

ELK RIDGE PARK

The mudroom near the back door is a place to store gear and wash up, with the laundry facilities located conveniently in the room. It could do double duty as a powder room with the addition of a toilet.

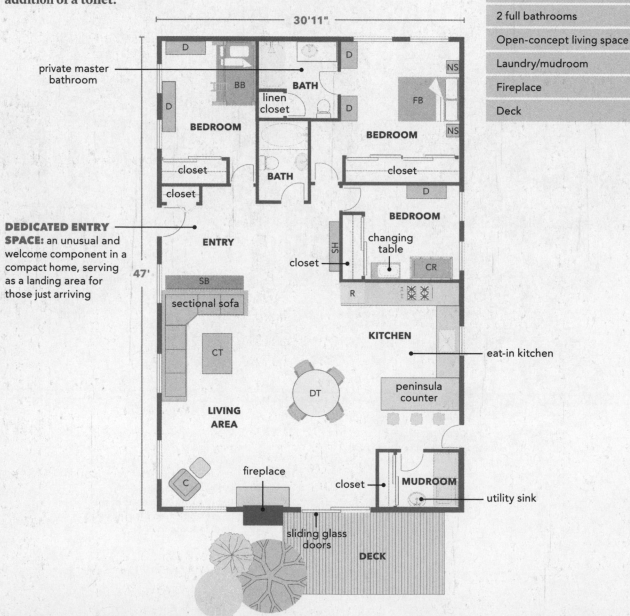

private master bathroom

DEDICATED ENTRY SPACE: an unusual and welcome component in a compact home, serving as a landing area for those just arriving

eat-in kitchen

fireplace

closet

utility sink

sliding glass doors

PITCHED ROOF: could accommodate solar panels if oriented to the south

SIMPLE, UNFUSSY DESIGN AND STYLE: keep the construction economical and allow the home to integrate well into a range of locales

THREE EXITS: combine with ample windows to help the home radiate a sense of active engagement with the outdoors

HIGH POINT

With two decks and a hot tub, this design emphasizes outdoor living. The front entry shelters beneath the roof, protecting visitors during inclement weather, while the open-concept living space invites conviviality between the chef and the rest of the household.

Features

1,420 square feet

3 bedrooms

2 full bathrooms

Open-concept living space

Fireplace

Multiple decks

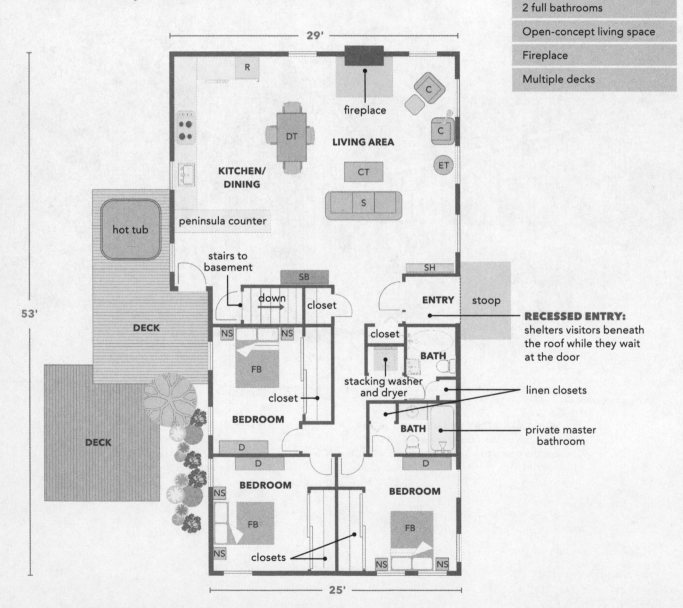

29'

R

fireplace

C

C

DT

ET

LIVING AREA

KITCHEN/
DINING

CT

S

hot tub

peninsula counter

53'

stairs to
basement

SB

down

closet

SH

ENTRY

stoop

DECK

NS   NS

closet

BATH

RECESSED ENTRY:
shelters visitors beneath
the roof while they wait
at the door

FB

closet

stacking washer
and dryer

linen closets

DECK

closet

BEDROOM

BATH

private master
bathroom

D

D

D

NS

BEDROOM

BEDROOM

NS

FB

FB

NS

closets

NS   NS

25'

MASONRY FIREPLACE: can efficiently heat the entirety of the open-concept living area

DOUBLE DECKS: create an inviting outdoor living space, complete with hot tub; they can be as large or as small as you're inclined to have them

WEST VALLEY

With its open, high-ceilinged living space, this house feels much bigger than its 1,430 square feet. The design has great potential for energy efficiency: If oriented so the back of the house faces south, it has possible passive solar applications; if the front of the house faces southward, the roof over the bedroom wing could support solar panels.

Features

1,430 square feet

3 bedrooms

1 full and 1 three-quarter bathroom

Open-concept living space

Fireplace

Multiple decks

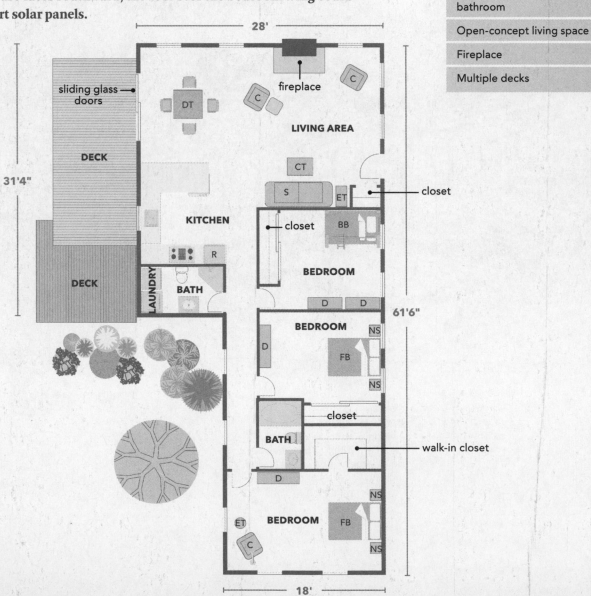

28'

fireplace

sliding glass doors

DT

C

C

DECK

LIVING AREA

31'4"

CT

S   ET

closet

KITCHEN

closet

BB

R

BEDROOM

61'6"

LAUNDRY

BATH

DECK

D   D

BEDROOM

D

NS

FB

NS

closet

BATH

walk-in closet

D

NS

BEDROOM

FB

ET

C

NS

18'

HIGH ROOFLINE: allows for a cathedral ceiling over the main living space

PITCHED ROOF: could accommodate solar panels if oriented to the south

HIGH WALL OF WINDOWS: brings light to the main living space, with possible passive solar applications

BEDROOM WING: keeps the sleeping quarters separate from the bustle of the main living space

KING'S GAP

This compact house puts an emphasis on living space, with the entire first floor given over to a great room. One side of the roof is pitched to take advantage of the sunlight with photovoltaic panels.

Features
832 square feet
2 bedrooms
1 full bathroom
Open-concept living space
Fuel-burning stove
Deck

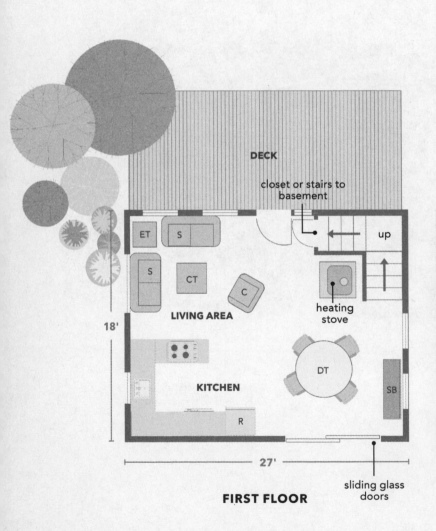

DECK

closet or stairs to basement

up

ET S

S

CT

C

LIVING AREA

heating stove

18'

KITCHEN

DT

SB

R

27'

sliding glass doors

FIRST FLOOR

NS

down

D

FB

closet

BEDROOM

closet

LAUNDRY

NS

FB

BEDROOM

D

BATH

closet

SECOND FLOOR

ROOFLINE: is designed to accommodate solar panels and should be oriented to the south

SMALL FOOTPRINT: works well for small or odd-shaped lots, integrating all the traditional amenities of home in an extremely compact space

LARGE LANDSCAPING ELEMENTS: help balance any stretch of exterior wall without windows, whether due to privacy concerns or, as here, to interior cabinetry

CLARION CROSSING

This is a small, efficient house, perfect as a first home or vacation home. The double decks offer an ample view behind the house, making this a good choice for a waterfront or hilltop property.

Features

920 square feet	
2 bedrooms	
1 full and 1 half bathroom	
Open-concept living space	
Fireplace	
Double decks	

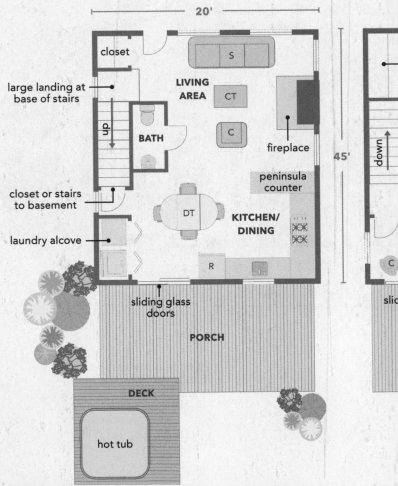

20'

45'

closet

large landing at base of stairs

LIVING AREA

S

CT

C

up

BATH

fireplace

closet or stairs to basement

peninsula counter

DT

KITCHEN/ DINING

laundry alcove

R

sliding glass doors

PORCH

DECK

hot tub

FIRST FLOOR

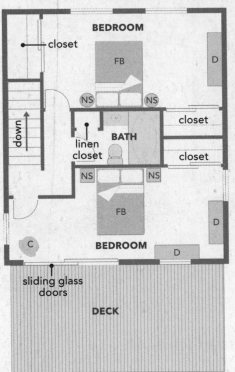

closet

BEDROOM

FB

D

down

NS

NS

linen closet

BATH

closet

closet

NS

NS

FB

C

D

BEDROOM

D

sliding glass doors

DECK

SECOND FLOOR

LOW-PITCHED ROOF: is best suited for climates that don't receive much snowfall

CLERESTORY WINDOWS: bring light to the bedroom and can be opened in warm weather for natural ventilation

SECOND-FLOOR DECK: for the adjacent bedroom is a great private spot for enjoying the view

PINE GROVE

With its circular traffic flow on the first floor, this is a great house for young kids, with plenty of outdoor living space for running around. Either of the two spacious upstairs bedrooms could accommodate bunk beds.

Features

950 square feet
2 bedrooms
1 full and 1 half bathroom
Fireplace
Multiple decks

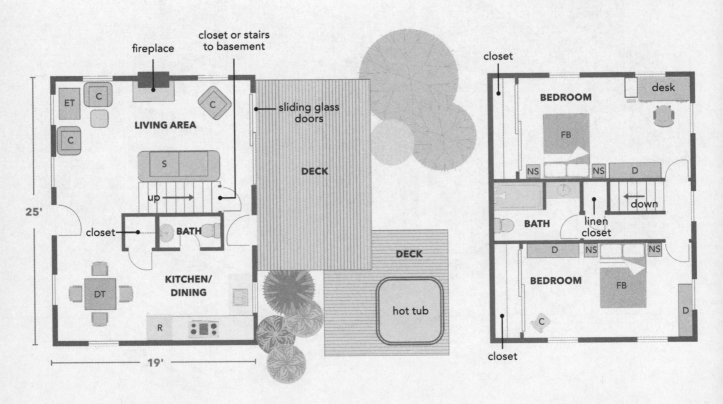

FIRST FLOOR

SECOND FLOOR

STEEP ROOF PITCH: allows room for storage space under the rafters

DOUBLE DECKS: create an inviting outdoor living space, complete with hot tub

RACCOON CREEK

This is a comfortable, inviting home for a single person or couple, with a single bedroom and a gracious morning room or reading area on the second floor. The open concept of the first floor makes it ideal for entertaining guests.

Features

956 square feet

1 bedroom

1 full and 1 half bathroom

Open-concept living space

Second-floor reading area

Deck

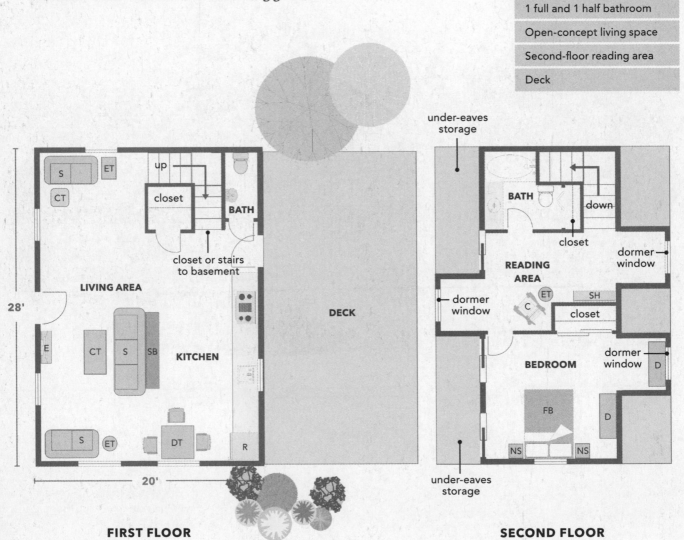

FIRST FLOOR

SECOND FLOOR

DORMERS: are ideal spots for cushioned window seats in the second-floor reading area

SLOPED SECOND-FLOOR CEILINGS: combine with the modest footprint and dormered windows to lend the home a classic Cape sensibility

BACKYARD DECK: can easily be expanded to accommodate a water feature, hot tub, or container garden; its size and shape are limited only by the parameters of the building lot

DENTON HILL

A wall of windows and skylights frame a light well in the front of this home, making the living room and second-floor reading area bright and inviting even on cloudy days. Orient the pitched roof toward the south to accommodate solar panels.

Features
979 square feet
1 bedroom
1 full and 1 half bathroom
Second-floor reading area
Deck

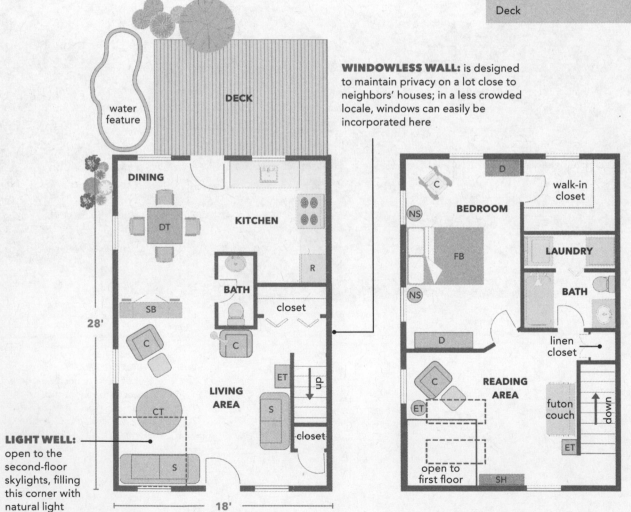

WINDOWLESS WALL: is designed to maintain privacy on a lot close to neighbors' houses; in a less crowded locale, windows can easily be incorporated here

LIGHT WELL: open to the second-floor skylights, filling this corner with natural light

water feature

DECK

DINING

KITCHEN

DT

R

BATH

SB

closet

C

CT

ET

LIVING AREA

S

up

closet

S

28'

18'

BEDROOM

C

NS

D

walk-in closet

FB

LAUNDRY

NS

BATH

D

linen closet

C

ET

READING AREA

futon couch

down

ET

open to first floor

SH

ET

FIRST FLOOR

SECOND FLOOR

PITCHED ROOF: is designed to accommodate solar panels and should be oriented to the south

SKYLIGHTS: at the top of the light well transform the space into a true column of natural light

HIGH COLUMN OF WINDOWS: forms the wall of the light well, filling the living and reading areas with natural light

SUGAR RUN

A compact take on a classic colonial, with generous storage closets in the bedrooms. Though the smaller bedroom is designed for kids, it would also work well as a master bedroom, with a fireplace using the chimney that runs up the outside wall.

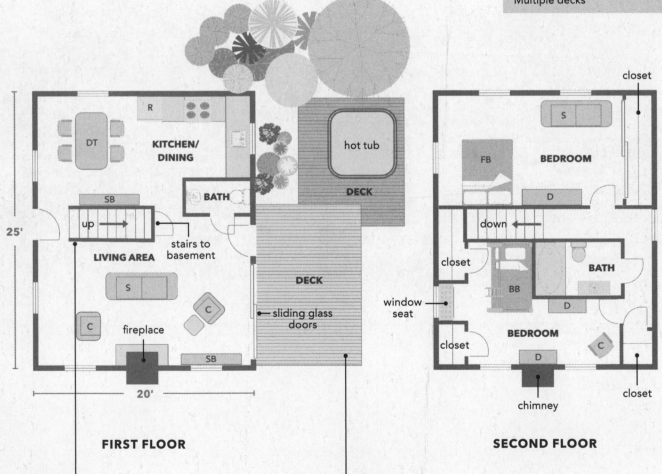

25'

20'

R

DT

KITCHEN/DINING

SB

up

stairs to basement

BATH

hot tub

DECK

LIVING AREA

S

C

C

fireplace

SB

DECK

sliding glass doors

FIRST FLOOR

closet

S

FB

BEDROOM

D

down

closet

window seat

BB

BATH

D

closet

BEDROOM

D

C

chimney

closet

SECOND FLOOR

PEGS OR HOOKS: can be set along the stairwell wall for holding coats and outdoor gear

DOUBLE DECKS: create an inviting outdoor living space, complete with hot tub

TRANSOM WINDOWS: set over the door lets in light without impinging upon privacy

TRADITIONAL COLONIAL EXTERIOR: complete with a stone chimney and shutters helps the home integrate well with an existing suburban neighborhood

TYLER CREEK

Walls of windows flood the home with natural light, while solar panels mounted on the roof above convert that light to energy. With three full bedrooms, this design graciously accommodates a good-size family in a compact footprint.

<table>
<tr><td>

Features

</td></tr>
<tr><td>

1,052 square feet

</td></tr>
<tr><td>

3 bedrooms

</td></tr>
<tr><td>

1 three-quarter and 1 half bathroom

</td></tr>
<tr><td>

Open-concept living space

</td></tr>
</table>

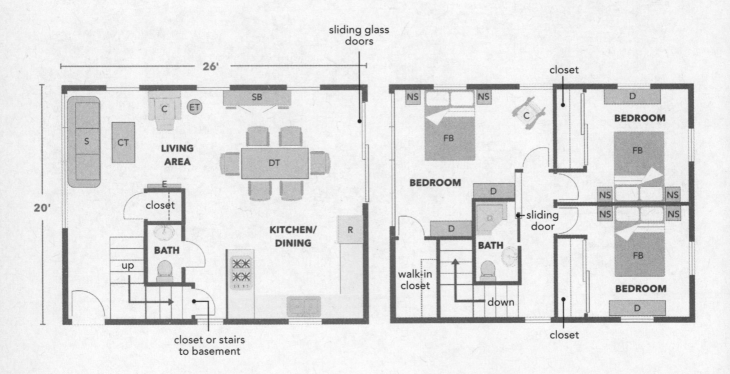

sliding glass doors

26'

20'

SB

C   ET

S   CT

LIVING AREA

DT

E

closet

KITCHEN/ DINING

R

BATH

up

closet or stairs to basement

FIRST FLOOR

closet

NS   NS

C

closet

D

BEDROOM

FB

BEDROOM

FB

D

NS   NS

sliding door

NS   NS

D

BATH

FB

walk-in closet

down

BEDROOM

D

closet

SECOND FLOOR

PITCHED ROOF: is designed to accommodate solar panels and should be oriented to the south

LONG BANKS OF WINDOWS: bring natural light to the first-floor living area and second-floor master bedroom

KITCHEN WINDOW: faces the front yard, an orientation that is unusual but perhaps desirable for a family whose children's activities will be focused in front of the house, such as if the house abuts a park

OLD BULL

This compact plan allows a surprising amount of light into the core of the home while preserving privacy. The galley kitchen provides generous countertops.

COAT PEGS: would work well on the closet wall, opposite the door

GLASS BLOCK WALL: allows natural light to penetrate master bedroom while preserving privacy

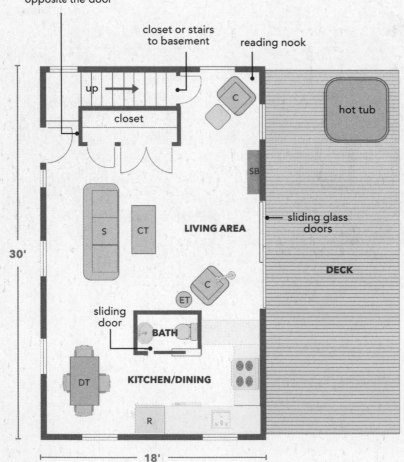

FIRST FLOOR

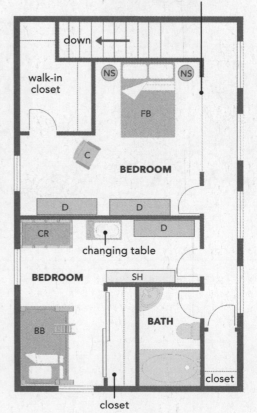

SECOND FLOOR

CLERESTORY WINDOWS:
bring light to the bedrooms and
can be opened in warm weather
for natural ventilation

FRONT ENTRY: opens onto an
oversize closet, with plenty of space
for coats, shoes, and outdoor gear

EXPANSIVE BACKYARD DECK:
can easily accommodate a hot tub or
container garden

MARCH CREEK

The loft design of this small house makes it feel bigger than it is, and it could easily be adapted to post-and-beam construction. With its open concept, the home could easily be entirely heated with a woodstove in the main living area.

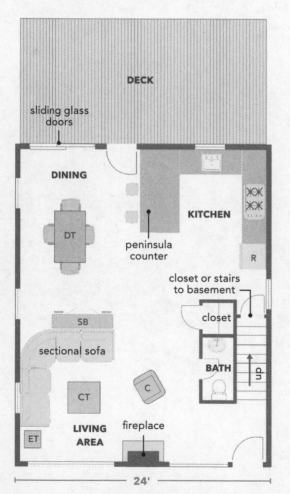

DECK

sliding glass doors

DINING

KITCHEN

DT

peninsula counter

R

closet or stairs to basement

closet

SB

sectional sofa

BATH

up

CT

C

ET

LIVING AREA

fireplace

24'

30'

FIRST FLOOR

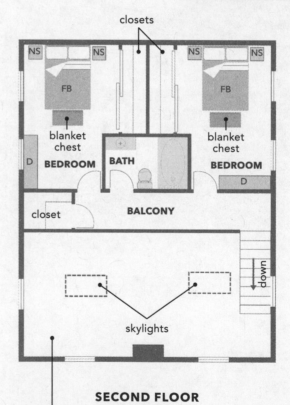

closets

NS   NS   NS   NS

FB   FB

blanket chest   blanket chest

D

BEDROOM   BATH   BEDROOM

D

closet   BALCONY

down

skylights

SECOND FLOOR

OPEN LEVEL: gives the house a spacious and airy feeling, with a cathedral ceiling in the first-floor living area

SKYLIGHTS: provide natural light and draw the eye upward to the cathedral ceiling, enhancing the spacious feel of the main living area

PICTURE WINDOWS: provide an unobstructed view toward the front of the house

MASONRY FIREPLACE: is exposed for two full stories on the interior and can be a striking centerpiece of the home's design

WARRIORS PATH

A surprisingly spacious small house with a third-floor loft. The glassed-in foyer protects the living space from cold and wind when the front door is opened, while still allowing natural light into the core of the building.

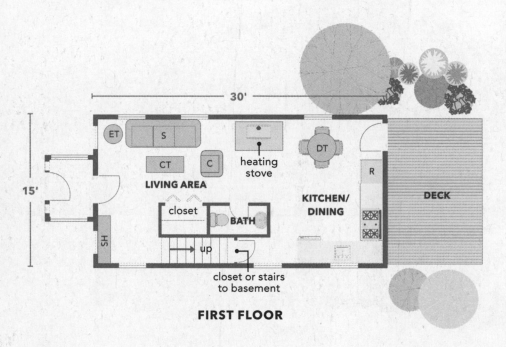

FIRST FLOOR

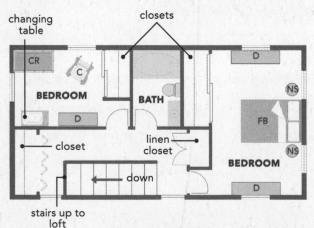

SECOND FLOOR

THIRD FLOOR

SKYLIGHT: becomes a portal to the sky through the high, sloped ceiling of the front bedroom

PITCHED ROOF: could support solar panels if oriented to the south

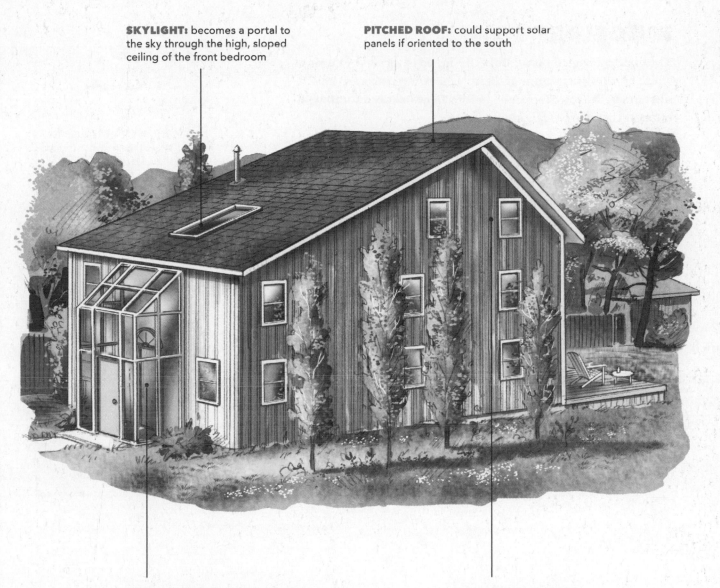

GLASSED-IN ENTRY: creates a striking foyer and opens up the potential for passive solar gain

THIRD-FLOOR LOFT: is a private bedroom nook with its own bathroom

RIDGEWAY

The glassed, angled bump-out is designed to focus a great view, while allowing maximum light into the living space and an upstairs bedroom. The pitched roof can be oriented southward to allow the use of solar panels.

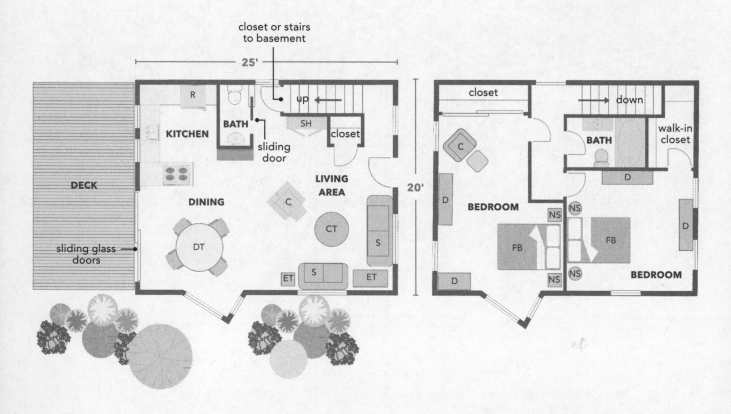

FIRST FLOOR

SECOND FLOOR

PITCHED ROOF: could accommodate solar panels if oriented to the south

ANGLED BUMP-OUT: is a striking architectural detail and fills the home with natural light

MORAINE RIDGE

This is a great design if your focus is on outdoor living. The living space wraps around the deck, connecting the outdoors to the indoors, while a screened gazebo allows for three-season outdoor dining.

Features

1,185 square feet

2 bedrooms

1 full and 1 three-quarter bathroom

Open-concept living space

Deck with gazebo

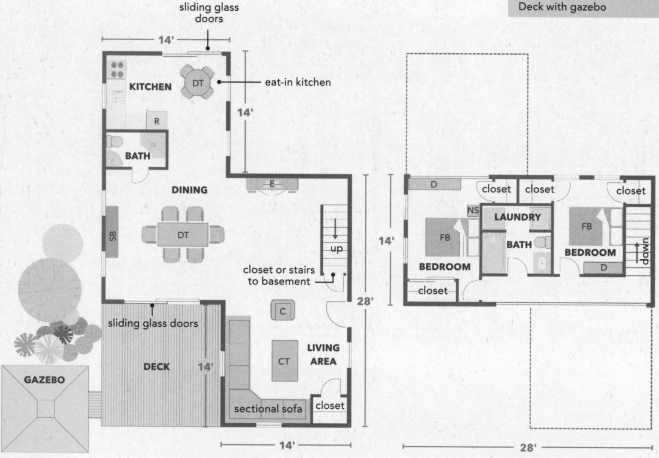

sliding glass doors

14'

KITCHEN

DT — eat-in kitchen

14'

R

BATH

DINING

SB

DT

E

up

closet or stairs to basement

C

CT

LIVING AREA

sliding glass doors

DECK   14'

GAZEBO

sectional sofa   closet

14'

28'

14'

FIRST FLOOR

D   closet   closet   closet

NS   LAUNDRY

FB   BATH

FB   BEDROOM

BEDROOM   D

closet

down

14'

28'

SECOND FLOOR

CLERESTORY WINDOWS: bring light to the upstairs hall and can be opened for natural ventilation

GAZEBO: could be screened for enjoyable three-season outdoor dining

DECK: is sheltered by the house on two sides, making it a very private outdoor living space

BELL GROVE

With its simple rectangular dimensions, this house could easily be built with structural insulated panels, which would speed construction and support energy efficiency. One side of the roof is elongated to accommodate a full array of solar panels.

Features

1,200 square feet

2 bedrooms

1 full and 1 three-quarter bathroom

Open-concept living space

Deck

FIRST FLOOR

SECOND FLOOR

ELONGATED ROOF: is designed to accommodate a large array of solar panels

CLASSIC RECTANGULAR SHAPE: allows the use of structural insulated panels (SIPs) in construction, lowering costs and supporting energy efficiency and insulative capabilities

HEMLOCK RUN

This is a modern take on the raised ranch. The main level accommodates the living quarters, with a generous deck and clerestory windows for natural lighting. The lower level houses the garage and can be finished, as shown here, to add 830 square feet to the living space. This is an ideal design for areas where the bedrock is close to the surface and digging a cellar would be expensive.

Features
1,210 square feet
2 bedrooms
1 full and 1 half bathroom
Large lower-level room
Deck

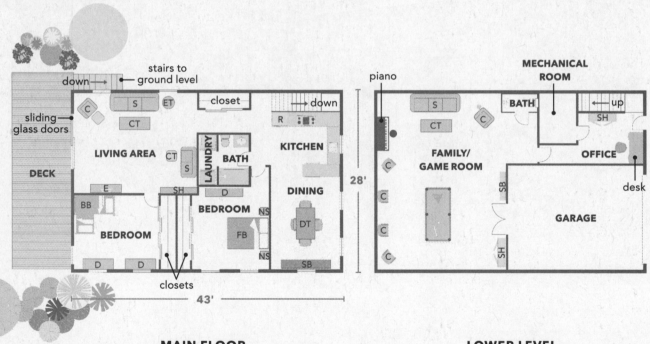

MAIN FLOOR   **LOWER LEVEL**

CLERESTORY WINDOWS: wrap around the front of the home, suffusing the interior with natural light

SECOND-STORY DECK: is a peaceful spot for enjoying a great view

ABOVEGROUND LOWER LEVEL: is ideal for a garage, family room, in-law quarters, studio, or shop

RAVENSBURG

Operable skylights and clerestory windows enhance natural ventilation in warmer weather, while the wrap-around deck offers 270-degree views. With a bedroom and bathroom on the first floor, this is an ideal design for empty nesters who want to have guest rooms for visiting family, or the downstairs bedroom could be converted to a home office.

Features

1,210 square feet

3 bedrooms

1 full and 1 three-quarter bathroom

Open-concept living space

Second-floor balcony

Wrap-around deck

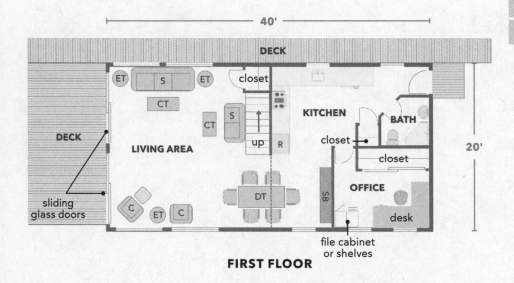

FIRST FLOOR

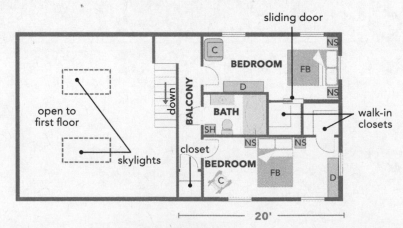

SECOND FLOOR

CLERESTORY WINDOWS: bring light to the interior and can be opened in warm weather for natural ventilation

WRAP-AROUND DECK: is a great spot for taking in a grand view, making this a good design for the waterfront or hilltop

MAIN LIVING AREA: is surrounded by glass on all sides, complemented by skylights above

SWATERA

The glass atrium brings light into the living area and two of the bedrooms, making this a good design for a heavily wooded lot, where natural light will be minimal.

Features

1,221 square feet

3 bedrooms

1 full and 1 half bathroom

Open-concept living space

Two-story solar atrium

Multiple decks

PANTRY STORAGE:
is located just off
the kitchen in a deep
cabinet; sliding shelves
set on runners would
make it easy to access all
the goods stored here

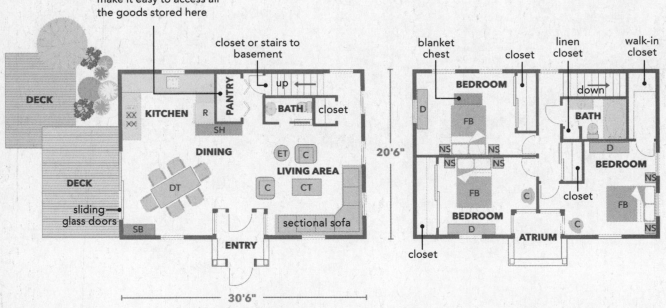

FIRST FLOOR

SECOND FLOOR

SOLAR ATRIUM: forms a two-story glass light well, drawing natural light into the interior

DOUBLE DECKS: create an inviting outdoor living space

LAUREL MOUNTAIN

The glass atrium allows natural light into the first floor and an upstairs bedroom; this atrium could be oriented to the south for passive solar applications. Each bedroom has its own full bathroom, a great convenience for families with children.

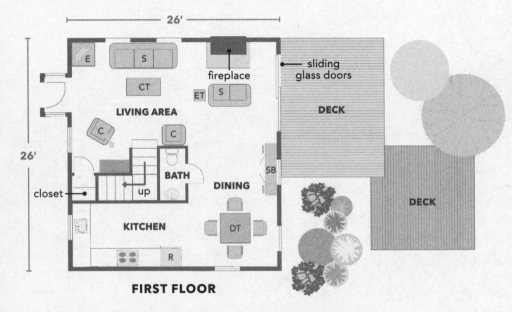

FIRST FLOOR

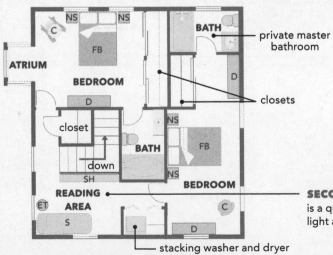

SECOND FLOOR

SECOND-FLOOR READING AREA: is a quiet retreat with plenty of natural light and a large bookshelf

PITCHED ROOF: could accommodate solar panels on whichever side faces south

SOLAR ATRIUM: draws natural light into the first-floor living area and is a bright and cheerful nook for the front bedroom on the second floor

DOUBLE DECKS: create an inviting outdoor living space

LITTLE BUFFALO

A modern concept designed to take advantage of an amazing landscape. Essentially each end of the home offers 270-degree views. This is a good design for a hilltop home, or for one of the long, narrow lots that are typical along the waterfront. Each bedroom has its own full bathroom.

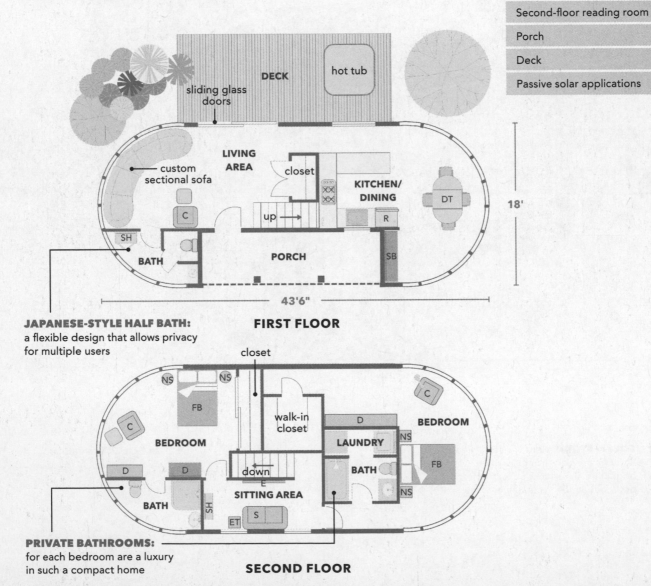

JAPANESE-STYLE HALF BATH:
a flexible design that allows privacy
for multiple users

FIRST FLOOR

PRIVATE BATHROOMS:
for each bedroom are a luxury
in such a compact home

SECOND FLOOR

RAISED-RIB METAL ROOF:
combines with the glass walls for a
modern, almost post-industrial style

PORCH: offers a recessed
and sheltered entry for visitors

GLASS WALLS: offer panoramic
views from both levels of the house,
making this an ideal home for a
waterfront or hilltop

LITTLE PINE

The deck in this design offers good privacy from neighbors, surrounded on two sides by the home's exterior walls and with a gazebo on a third side. With the glass sliding doors to the deck oriented to the south, this would be a good passive solar design.

Features

1,380 square feet

3 bedrooms

1 full, 1 three-quarter, and 1 half bathroom

Open-concept living space

Deck with gazebo

Passive solar applications

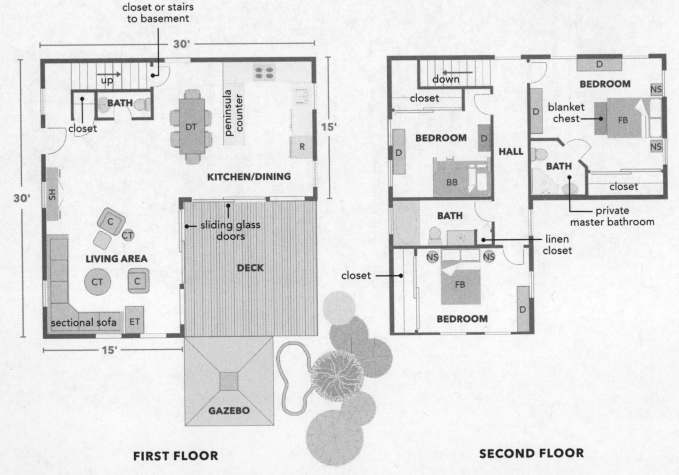

FIRST FLOOR

SECOND FLOOR

MISMATCHED ROOFLINES: where the kitchen wing meets the main section of the house allows for clerestory windows to be tucked beneath the higher roofline, shedding light into the upstairs hall

BACKYARD FOCUS: is the dominant feature of the first floor, making this a good design for a family that spends a lot of time out in the yard

DECK: is sheltered by the house on two sides, making it a private outdoor living space

LAUREL SUMMIT

With a covered porch on either end of the house, this home encourages enjoyment of the outdoors and can be situated to take advantage of a great view. One of the upstairs bedrooms can be fitted with a small stove.

Features

1,384 square feet

2 bedrooms

2 full and 1 half bathrooms

Open-concept living space

Fuel-burning stove

Two porches

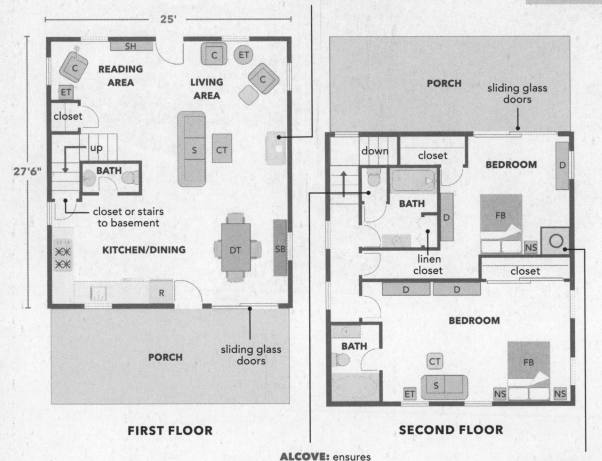

HEATING STOVE: could easily be replaced by a masonry fireplace to enhance the ambience

ALCOVE: ensures privacy for the toilet while still allowing free use of the sink

CHIMNEY: could be tapped into for a small stove in this second-floor bedroom

FIRST FLOOR

SECOND FLOOR

SECOND-FLOOR PORCH: is a fresh-air private retreat, accessible only from the back bedroom

PITCHED ROOF: could support solar panels if oriented to the south

FIRST-FLOOR PORCH: is deeply sheltered by the house above, providing shade and helping to keep the interior cool

LINN RUN

This home features spacious bedrooms and a large living space. The Pullman-style kitchen maximizes counter space in a small footprint. Screened on two sides by the house, the deck encourages outdoor living, while its glass sliding doors bring natural light into the main living area.

Features

1,384 square feet

2 bedrooms

2 full and 1 half bathrooms

Fireplace

Deck with gazebo

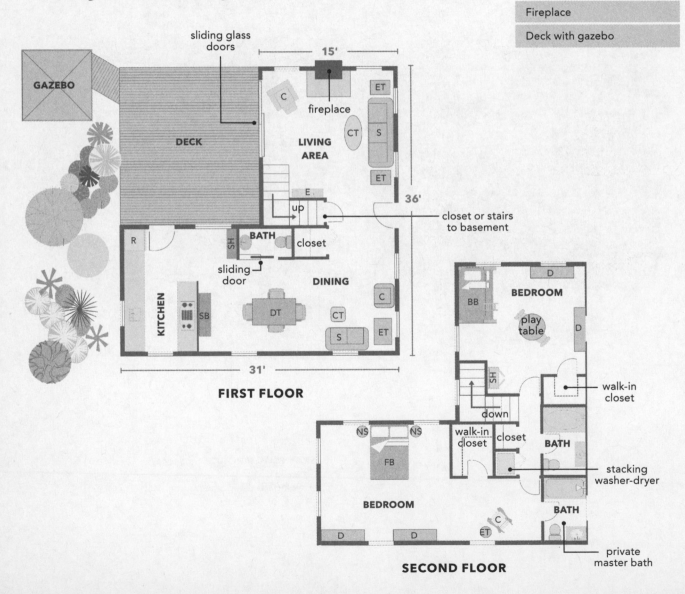

sliding glass doors

GAZEBO

15'

fireplace

DECK

LIVING AREA

ET

CT

S

ET

36'

E

up

closet or stairs to basement

BATH

SH

closet

sliding door

DINING

C

CT

ET

S

R

KITCHEN

SB

DT

31'

FIRST FLOOR

D

BEDROOM

BB

play table

D

SH

down

walk-in closet

walk-in closet

closet

BATH

NS

NS

FB

stacking washer-dryer

BEDROOM

D

D

ET

C

BATH

private master bath

SECOND FLOOR

PITCHED ROOF: enables a sloping ceiling in the upstairs bedrooms, with the beds tucked under the lower end

DECK: is sheltered by the house on two sides, making it a very private outdoor living space

UPPER PINE BOTTOM

This flexible design works well in a suburban neighborhood, with an attached garage that could easily be converted to a home office, studio, or in-law quarters, depending on the homeowners' needs.

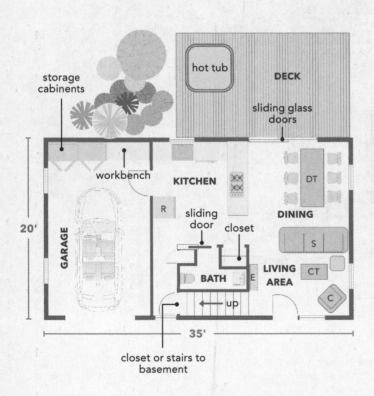

storage cabinents

workbench

FIRST FLOOR

closet or stairs to basement

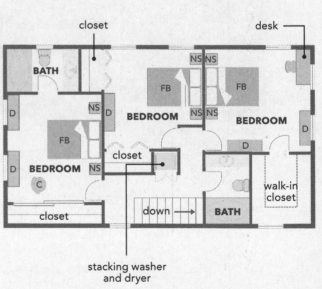

closet

desk

stacking washer and dryer

SECOND FLOOR

WINDOWS: on the garage-side wall could easily be enlarged or doubled for more light and ventilation

INCORPORATED GARAGE: is a convenient and traditional feature in suburban areas, providing sheltered interior passage from the car to the home

YELLOW CREEK

The long, narrow design of this house lends itself nicely to the typically long, narrow lots in urban and waterfront neighborhoods. One end of the home is almost entirely glass, to take advantage of a great view or for passive solar applications.

Features

1,400 square feet

3 bedrooms

1 full and 1 half bathroom

Fireplace

Passive solar applications

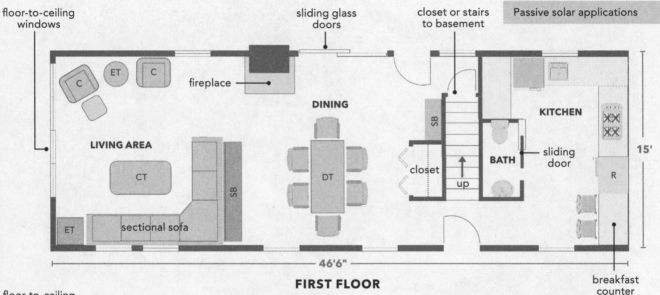

floor-to-ceiling windows

sliding glass doors

closet or stairs to basement

fireplace

DINING

KITCHEN

LIVING AREA

SB

BATH

sliding door

closet

CT

up

SB

R

ET

sectional sofa

DT

15'

46'6"

breakfast counter

FIRST FLOOR

floor-to-ceiling windows

chimney

closet

closet

BEDROOM

BATH

BEDROOM

down

FB

LAUNDRY

FB

closet

BEDROOM

walk-in closet

walk-in closet

SECOND FLOOR

INWARD-ANGLED ROOF AND RAISED-RIB SIDING: give the home a modernist style, complemented by the great glass wall at one end

WALL OF WINDOWS: brings light and a great view to the main living space and upstairs bedroom, with possible passive solar applications

FAWN GROVE

This version of a classic colonial features independent in-law quarters, which could also be set up as a rental unit. At just over 1,400 square feet, it packs a lot of living into a compact footprint.

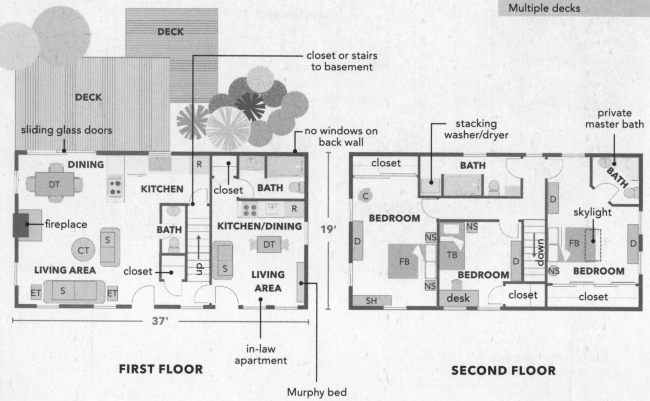

FIRST FLOOR

SECOND FLOOR

SKYLIGHT: opens into the cathedral ceiling of the master suite

DOUBLE DECKS: create an inviting outdoor living space

IN-LAW APARTMENT: is tucked into the first floor and allows multigenerational yet still independent cohabitation

MOUNT ALTO

With its sunroom, expanses of windows, and double decks, this is another design with a focus on outdoor living. The sunroom, if oriented southward, allows for passive solar heating.

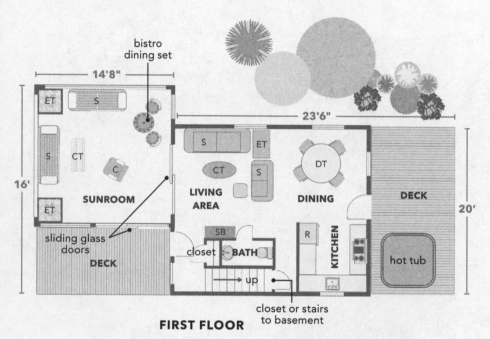

FIRST FLOOR

SECOND FLOOR

BANKS OF WINDOWS: provide striking views, lots of natural light, and good ventilation

SUNROOM: effectively doubles the size of the living area, yet it can be closed off for privacy or to conserve heat in colder weather

FRONT DECK: defines the entry to the house, offering an extended, low-level transition from outdoors to indoors

HOLLY SPRING

This is an ideal design for a townhouse, with the back walls shared with one or more adjoining properties. (If the house is freestanding, you could also fill those walls with windows.) Porches on both levels offer a great view of the water, the ski slopes, or whatever landscape you dream of building on.

Features

1,450 square feet
3 bedrooms
1 full and 1 half bathroom
Two porches
Patio

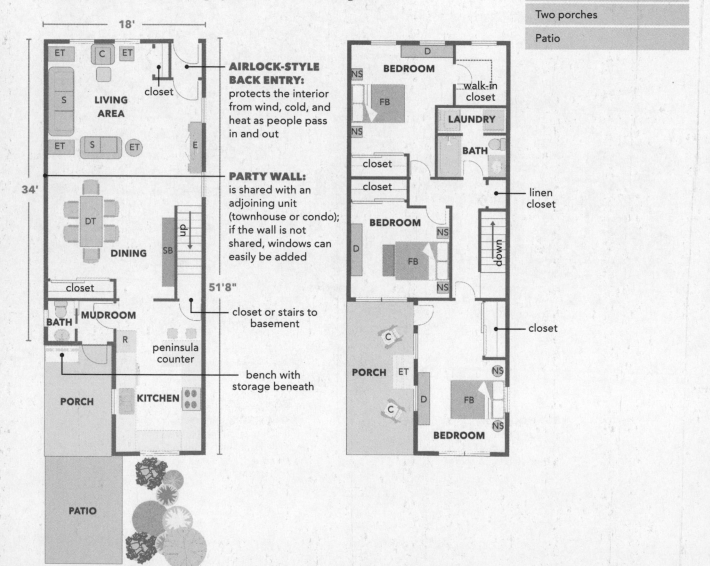

AIRLOCK-STYLE BACK ENTRY: protects the interior from wind, cold, and heat as people pass in and out

PARTY WALL: is shared with an adjoining unit (townhouse or condo); if the wall is not shared, windows can easily be added

closet or stairs to basement

bench with storage beneath

peninsula counter

FIRST FLOOR

SECOND FLOOR

linen closet

closet

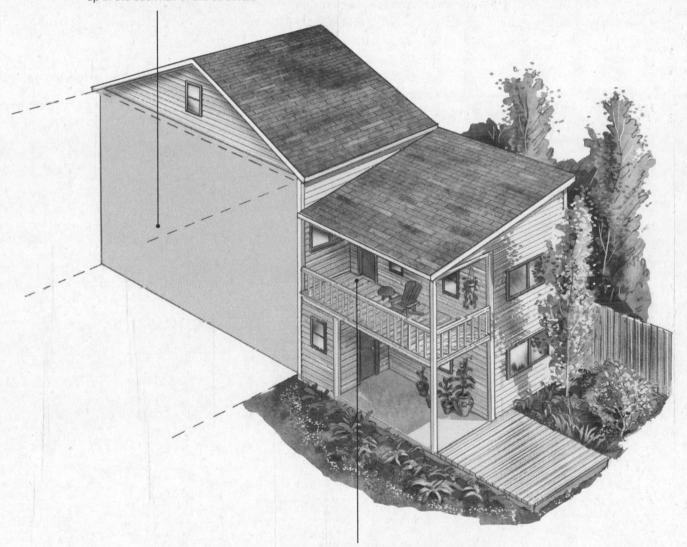

NEIGHBORING UNITS: share a party wall with this townhouse design, joining up in the back half of the structure

SECOND-STORY PORCH: is a private outdoor nook for the front bedroom

CHAPTER 2

DESIGN: KEY FACTORS FOR SMALL SPACES

THIS BOOK IS ABOUT SMALL —
THAT IS, SMALL HOUSES. WHILE
JUST A COUPLE OF DECADES
AGO VERY BIG HOUSES WERE
BEING BUILT AT AN ASTONISHING
RATE, THE AVERAGE HOME SIZE
IS NOW SHRINKING BACK DOWN.
WHY? IN PART, THERE'S BEEN A
STYLISTIC PUSH AGAINST THE
IDEA OF THE "McMANSION."

Today's aspiring homeowners tend to prioritize quality and craftsmanship over size, and they generally allocate their funds accordingly. It's also true that energy, material, land, and labor costs are rising, and consumers are more aware of the environmental and ecological concerns involved with the construction and maintenance of a home. Given these considerations, building small makes sense.

With the downsizing trend has come increasing pressure to improve the design of the "new" small house. Good home design relies heavily on ergonomics, the science of designing our built environment — from the home itself to its furnishings and appliances — to fit the function, movement, and comfort of the human body. Ergonomics is a particularly important consideration in the design of small spaces. Our satisfaction with a compact home is linked directly to how well the space is designed for our needs and comfort. In this chapter, we'll take a look at the particular areas of concern in the design of a compact house.

ERGONOMICS VERSUS STYLE

There are two ways to look at a house design: a floor plan and an elevation. The floor plan usually determines the square footage of the building and the relationships among its parts (the kitchen, bathroom, bedrooms, and so on). The elevation is the facade of the house, or what you see from the outside.

As a general rule, floor plans are about ergonomics, or the ways in which people move in and inhabit the space. Elevations are generally about style. Any small-house floor plan may have a dozen different elevations that would work with it, just as any elevation may work well with a dozen different floor plans. Each pairing of floor plan and elevation yields a unique melding of style and ergonomics.

These two concepts — ergonomics and style — begin with the basic structure of the home (the floor plan and elevation) and carry on down through the smallest details. Ergonomics guides the placement and size of the furniture, while style determines the look and character. Ergonomics guides the selection of flooring in the kitchen, while style determines the exact material and color. As design concepts, ergonomics and style are separate considerations, each guided by different concerns and principles. In good home design, however, they are inextricably linked, each shaping the other in the development of a home that suits the particular needs and tastes of the individual homeowner.

The generic floor plan of a traditional compact home encompasses a rectangular exterior. Ergonomics will guide how the interior is divided into unique spaces — and those divisions will vary depending on personal needs and aesthetic.

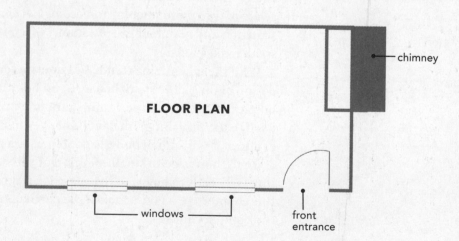

FLOOR PLAN

chimney

windows

front entrance

Basic elevation

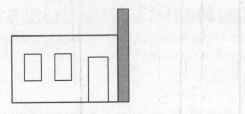

The elevation shows the style the designer envisions for the home. But when you're looking at a plan, keep in mind that the style is mutable; without changing the floor plan, you can significantly change the look of the house.

Roofline and window options

Varying the roofline and windows yields an almost limitless number of designs, even for a simple rectangular home.

 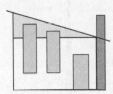 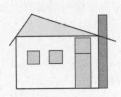

  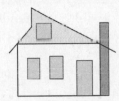

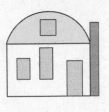 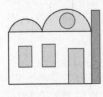 

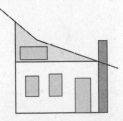  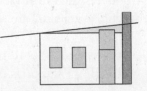

GOOD HOUSE DESIGN

In a home, good design functions on a number of levels, from ergonomics to aesthetics. It should satisfy the social, economic, and stylistic needs of the home's occupants. In particular, good design is:

Innovative, yet practical. It takes advantage of modern design principles and technology. It is not, however, innovative for the sake of being innovative. The innovation should add to the livability, function, and aesthetics of the house.

Aesthetics. A well-designed house should be beautiful (at least to the home's occupants).

Understandable. The house should have a human logic. Its spaces should flow naturally from one to the next, and its appliances and layout should allow it to function easily.

Unobtrusive. The house should fit well into its environment and not over-whelm its occupants with furnishings and landscaping. All the components of the house should feel married to one another.

Honest. The house does not make itself seem more innovative, powerful, or valuable than it really is. It has a directness and clarity of thought and expression.

Long-lasting. The design avoids kitschy or fashionable statements, which tend to be short-lived. Good house design should last for years and still be considered tasteful.

Given thorough consideration. The space is designed down to the last detail. No decision about any aspect, from the number of bathrooms to the lighting of the basement to the capacity of the dishwasher, is arbitrary.

Environmentally friendly. Good design minimizes waste and pollution. It allows a house to be environmentally friendly and as green as is practical.

Simple. Less is more. Good design concentrates on the essential aspects of the use and function of the home. The best solution is usually the simplest solution.

BASIC DESIGN PRINCIPLES FOR SMALL SPACES

When you're designing a small space, there are some general practices that will make the space work well and be eminently livable. Use these principles to guide the development of your home design, from the overall structure to the individual rooms, always keeping in mind the two main areas of focus: ergonomics and style.

Practice "Form Follows Function"

Especially in a small home, where ergonomics is key to comfortable living, every detail — from the layout of a room to its lighting to its wall color — must serve a purpose. And so your primary objective is to make each detail serve the function of the space. Every aspect of a kitchen, for example, should serve the greater purpose of cooking and serving food. If you want a convivial kitchen, one that invites people to join the cook and share in the meal preparation, then the kitchen must also be designed to function as a gathering place.

DESIGN VERSUS STYLE

Sometimes you'll hear the words *design* and *style* used interchangeably. They are not the same. Design deals with space, structure, and ergonomics. Design uses a logical structure to tackle problems of organizing living space so that it functions well and meets the needs of its inhabitants. Design is guided by ergonomics, economics (budget), the intended use and function of the space, and the inhabitants' personal sense of style.

That sense of style, itself just one consideration of the design, is an egocentric, personal aesthetic that guides what a structure looks and feels like. Style arises from our own experiences and creativity. Style determines whether we have a taste for Queen Anne, Bauhaus, midcentury modern, contemporary, or some fusion thereof. While good design determines every facet of a home, style is more a decorative perspective that permeates the structure. Of necessity, good design fuses style with appropriate technology to create a comfortable, functional, practical home. If your taste runs to American colonial, for example, you might furnish your home with chairs and tables of the colonial style, but you'd find a historically correct colonial kitchen almost impossible to work with. The same holds true for utilities and bathrooms — unless, of course, you actually prefer an outhouse.

And from these functions follows the form — from the layout, appliances, seating, and technology down to the atmosphere and aesthetic you want to feel in that kitchen.

This is not to say that a compact home is by nature utilitarian. Far from it. Just ask the Shakers, renowned for the beauty and craftsmanship of their buildings, furniture, and tools — and dogmatic believers in the philosophy of "form follows function." A home that is highly functional is all the more beautiful for being easy to live in.

Balance Flow and Boundaries

To feel comfortable, a home must exude a sense of both space (the ability to move freely and unhindered) and containment (each space's boundaries and purpose defined). Balancing the two concepts — flow and boundaries — allows a compact home to be comfortable and functional. Here we return to that concept of gestalt: the way in which the spaces work together determines the livability and functionality of the home.

Always start with the structure and, again, ergonomics. A small home should not comprise a series of small, walled-off rooms. But to avoid the feeling of a boxy warehouse — and yes, even a small home can feel *too* open — some definition of spaces within the home is needed. Not necessarily walls, mind you; a boundary can be as simple as a change in wall color or texture, or a ceiling beam that spans the divide between the living area and the eating area, or a unique tile floor that defines the expanse of the entry. A person moving from one space to the next should be able to see or feel the point of transition. Each room should also allow appropriate movement within it and into other spaces. From a living room, for example, you may want easy access to the kitchen or eating area — or perhaps even open access, with the living, eating, and kitchen areas open to one another. A bedroom, on the other hand, is more often a private space, enclosed by walls and given its own door, but you'll want to consider its proximity to the bathroom. If someone waking in the bedroom at nighttime has to cross through the seating area in the living room to get to the bathroom, the bedroom becomes less ergonomic — less comfortable and less easy to inhabit.

Scale Appropriately

One common problem with a small house is the scale of the furniture. Often people who have downsized into a smaller house find that they feel uncomfortable in their new home; it's hard to maneuver in and feels crowded. The

RV Innovations

Recent years have seen a boom in the design and building of recreational vehicles (RVs). It's now a very competitive market, with manufacturers vying to outdesign each other in terms of both technology and ergonomics. Since an RV is by nature compact, its components are compact as well, and many of these components translate well in a compact home. And since RVs are popular with an older population, comfort is an important factor in furniture design. So if you're looking for compact furniture, it may be worth your time to visit a local RV dealer and see the offerings.

I use some RV innovations in my own home. One of my favorites is a telescoping, folding towel rack. In the folded-up position it collapses against the wall and takes up little space. I mounted it on the bathroom wall and use it to hang wet clothes for drying. It also serves to hold extra towels for guests.

Less Is More

Several summers ago I was in Kyoto, Japan, during celebrations for a Buddhist festival. As part of that festival, most of the ancient Zen teahouses were open to the public. I was profoundly impacted by the minimalist design I saw there. The atriums of the teahouses were usually decorated with a simple low table supporting a porcelain vase with a single flower in it. One primary aspect of the Zen philosophy is that less is more. As the number of objects becomes fewer, the importance of each of the items increases. A single perfect flower is more powerful than all the flowers on the floats in the Rose Bowl Parade. I found I could grasp and appreciate the beauty of a simple flower far better than that of a rose-filled float. This idea can also be applied to living in small spaces.

reason? It's not the reduction in square footage. It's their furniture — it's too big. The furniture is scaled to fit a home twice the size of the one they're now living in. As a result, the people living in the smaller house are uncomfortable and unhappy — and beginning to rethink their move.

Furniture should be scaled to fit the space where it will be used. The idea that furniture has to be large to be comfortable is a common misconception. It is just not true. To be comfortable, furniture needs to be well designed, padded properly, and upholstered with an appropriate fabric. Size is a matter of appropriate scale, not comfort. The problem is that finding smaller-scale furniture can be a bit of a treasure hunt. Most suburban and mall-based furniture stores, being close to developments full of very large houses, stock only large-scale furniture. They are well aware of their market and cater to a certain kind of customer. A better resource for the owner of a compact home is an urban furniture store that caters to the taste and needs of apartment dwellers. Here you will find a very different aesthetic and scale in the furniture.

Housing in many parts of Europe (especially Scandinavia) and Japan is noticeably smaller than the housing we are accustomed to. This means that the furniture is smaller in scale, too. Furniture manufacturers from these countries would be good resources for owners of compact homes.

Of course, here in North America we can find many traditions of smaller houses in our own history. Early colonial through midcentury-modern furniture was scaled to fit small spaces. And if your taste runs to the eclectic, you may find mixing styles very satisfying. For example, Japanese (Zen) minimalism, Scandinavian modern, and American Shaker could all work very well together.

That said, balance spaces with both large and small furnishings. The use of small furnishings alone makes a space seem busy and cluttered. Don't avoid a couch just because it's bigger than a chair. A moderately sized couch — or perhaps a loveseat — can become the centerpiece of the living area, with smaller furniture to complement it.

Design around Focal Points

Rooms should have a focus. They can have a number of elements — windows, window treatments, furniture, artwork, carpeting and floor treatments, and so on — but they should spotlight a primary focus. It might be an interesting Persian carpet or a precious chair inherited from Grandma Ruth. Occupants of the room should be able to recognize the focus, whether because it is the most prominent thing in the room or because it is set off in a way that draws attention to it (on a mantel, for example, or in the center of a seating arrangement). And particularly for a small room, there should be just a single focus. When multiple focal points in a room compete, it makes the room feel unsettling and small.

Let Ergonomics Guide the Aesthetics

If the individual elements that we include in our home, such as the colors, textures, furnishings, and artwork, are the words that describe our aesthetic, design is the grammar that organizes this vocabulary into a coherent statement. Words can be just words, but with the right syntax, they can become poetry.

One of the common problems in small spaces that feel uncomfortable and crowded is how they are decorated. Most of these spaces end up too busy, with too many conflicting accents and oversize furniture. Here are a few suggestions to help you build a decorative style that expresses your personal aesthetic in a coherent, sensible, and functional way.

Walls. Start with the walls and work inward. Do you want the walls to be the focus of the room? If not, then an earth tone, neutral color, or pastel would be the appropriate finish. An unobtrusive wall color becomes the palette upon which a more colorful focal point — a richly colored rug, a bright painting, a favorite chair — is displayed. Conversely, furnishings in quiet colors will balance a room whose walls are painted a strikingly rich, warm orange.

Textures. Texture can be as important as color in creating comfortable, engaging, livable spaces. Texture can draw your eye around a space and focus your attention; you will see a textured surface before you see a smooth surface. But as with color, don't overdo the texture. Restoration contractors will sometimes remove the old plaster from a wall or chimney to expose the brick beneath it. The warm, worn brick makes a good textural accent on one wall, but you wouldn't want to live with the brick of the whole house exposed; it would become overwhelming and make the home seem smaller than it is.

Window treatments. The style of your window treatments should be dictated primarily by the degree of privacy you need. Privacy is of less concern in the living room of a country house than in, say, a city bedroom. So let privacy be your guiding concern, and then consider whether you want the window treatments to be the focal point of the room or an unobtrusive element.

Flooring. Floors can be tile, hardwood, wall-to-wall carpeting, or area rugs (and certainly other eclectic options exist). Again, ask yourself, what do I want people to see first when they enter this room? A beautiful Persian rug could be the focal point. Then the rest of the decorating in the room has to make this rug the center of interest. Colors that appear in the rug could be repeated or complemented in the colors of the walls, window treatments, or throw pillows. The important thing is that the rest of the room should not compete with this rug for visual attention. Choosing a palette of colors that are analogous to those of the rug will make the room function as a design whole. Then again, if the flooring is *not* the focal point, it should be of a simple texture and color, so that it won't compete with whatever you *have* chosen as the focal point.

Lighting. Your choice of recessed lighting, track lighting, pendants, sconces, accent lamps, or what-have-you (options abound) contributes to the design statement in the room. The primary concern is that the lighting be functional, illuminating areas as necessary: a living room chair needs adequate light for reading, for example, while a bathroom mirror needs lighting set over it, and a kitchen needs good lighting over each work area. Lighting can also be thought of as mood setting, adding to the overall atmosphere in the room.

Furniture. The size of the furniture and the number of pieces in a room are important considerations. Your taste may be antique, eclectic, contemporary, or period; that's your choice. But as discussed earlier (see page 118), the furniture must be scaled appropriately to the size of the room. In a compact home, that usually means compact furniture. Oversize furniture would make a compact home feel crowded and claustrophobic. Too much furniture in a room would produce the same result. How you arrange the furniture is a question of ergonomics: how will people use the space, and how can the furniture placement make that space comfortable and functional?

Remember: keep it simple. In most things, there's a natural tendency to evolve from simple to more complex. Knowing this, start out with the simple, allowing your home to naturally evolve into something more complex over time.

SIMPLIFYING

Go almost anywhere else in the world — Asia, Africa, Europe, Central America — and the prevalent philosophy in architecture and consumer culture is one of minimalism driven by need and ergonomics. What do we really need to live happy, fulfilled lives? It's surprisingly less than what most of us currently live with.

Any life coach, Zen master, motivational speaker, or other "good life" cheer-leader will tell you that it's the relationships we treasure, the experiences we navigate, and the mind-set we cultivate that lead to a happy, fulfilled life. And they're right, of course. But this book is about houses, and so here we're going to talk about our physical stuff: the tools, furnishings, accessories, and mementos that share our living space and, with any luck, make positive contri-butions to our lives.

Living well in a small space necessitates a certain prioritization of our belongings. We keep what we need and absolutely love; we lose the junk and the belongings we don't really use. For some of us such minimalism comes naturally — we have a spare aesthetic in our personal lives and tend not to accumulate belongings. For others, seasonal purging is a welcome relief, offer-ing us a chance to declutter our environment and bring clarity and space to our lives.

In a small home, space is at a premium, and we must use every inch of it with conscious intent. We'll talk more about space-saving storage and design features later, but the first step is simply to declutter. Evaluate your belong-ings with a steady, unbiased eye. Get rid of those tools and appliances that you don't use on a regular basis or, if they perform some irreplaceable but not-often-called-for function, set them aside to put in storage. Pare down your knickknacks and mementos to those that you truly love; if you're left with an overabundance, consider displaying them in rotation, switching out one set for another every few months. And for more good tips and advice, consult any of the many good books now available on decluttering and simplifying.

The benefit of simplifying is that you're able to demand good design and high quality from those things you do own. With any luck, that focus will bring all-around greater usefulness, ergonomic function, and enjoyment to your life.

USONIAN ARCHITECTURE

No discussion of the ergonomics of small spaces would be complete without a look at Usonian architecture. The name came from Frank Lloyd Wright, referring to his vision for building affordable, stylish homes for the common people of the United States (*U.S.-onian*), as an alternative to the term *American*. This style of architecture was born during the Great Depression and continues evolving, albeit under different names, even today.

In the mid-1930s, breaking from traditional colonial designs, Usonian architecture adopted the Bauhaus concept of "form follows function," basing home design on the needs of the occupants, which indeed were different from those of homeowners in decades past. Central heating systems, modern kitchens, and storage needs were evolving. Garages and carports were increasingly attached to homes, in contrast to carriage houses, which generally stood some distance from the house (due to the smell of the horses). And, pushing back against Victorian ideals, the Bauhaus movement favored the notion that good design was of itself aesthetically pleasing and didn't require additional ornamentation.

Usonian houses were built on one level, set on a concrete slab without an attic or cellar. Instead of having a number of small rooms, as was the contemporary fashion, they emphasized an open-concept living space, accompanied by small bedrooms. The kitchen, dining, and living rooms flowed together in one area. The houses were designed to minimize the need for doors and halls.

Many Usonian houses were among the first to utilize what have become standard elements of green architecture. Some made use of radiant floor heating, for example, with heating pipes embedded in the concrete slab. Some were designed with large roof overhangs, which made ventilation possible even in wet weather and, due to the seasonal change in the angle of the sun overhead, blocked midday summer sun from the house while still allowing in midday winter sun. As a result, these houses were naturally cooler in summer and warmer in winter. (Some of the earliest passive solar house designs were Usonian.) Many employed clerestory windows for natural lighting. Most made great use of wood, brick, stone, and other natural building materials and were designed to echo the forms of the local landscape.

Usonian architects also oriented the houses on their lots differently than in the past. They tended to build on odd-size or less desirable lots to keep costs affordable. They positioned houses farther back on the lots to help reduce the noise from automobile traffic on the street. And they relocated and reoriented entrances to accommodate the fact that occupants of the house and visitors would arrive by car.

The lives and lifestyles of Americans were in flux after the Second World War, and this new architecture met the needs of a modern culture. Many of the concepts developed in this architectural style have endured; they are very applicable to the needs of contemporary house design.

KITCHEN DESIGN

The kitchen is a central place in the modern home, having evolved from a utilitarian space for cooking to a more social space used not just for cooking but also for eating, socializing, homework, and other activities. To serve these expanded functions in a compact home, a kitchen must be designed to fit the specific needs and cooking style of the homeowners.

If you don't cook much, you can have a very compact kitchen, with a two-burner stove, compact fridge and other appliances, and minimal counter space, like you might find in a hotel suite. If you want a full-size kitchen, spending time up front looking at your options and planning the layout and style will ensure that your kitchen serves you well for years and years to come.

I grew up working in the kitchens of resorts in the Poconos of Pennsylvania and the Catskills and Adirondacks of New York. Though they fed hundreds at a time, these resorts had fairly small kitchens. Most of them were designed according to the classic kitchen "work triangle" philosophy: arranging the stove, refrigerator, and sink in an equilateral triangle, with the smallest practical distance between them. The idea was that the kitchen would be more efficient if the chefs did not have to move around a lot to prepare the meal. Everything they needed — utensils, pots, pans, seasonings — was available in their immediate work space. And everyone had their own station. Prep cooks, sous chefs, and line chefs could work efficiently without interfering with each other. There was an assembly line: the prep people passed the product along to the sous and line chefs, who passed it along to the servers. Chefs were able to produce meals efficiently and without undue fatigue in those kitchens.

Kitchen designers today debate whether the work triangle is an outmoded concept. With the preponderance of new appliances that have become standard (think of the microwave, toaster, coffeemaker, and countertop stand mixer), the fridge, oven, and sink are no longer the only elements in a kitchen. But the philosophy behind the work triangle — that all the primary appliances and workstations should be readily and efficiently accessible to the cook — remains irrefutable, and it becomes especially important in the design of a small kitchen. Which brings us back to the study of ergonomics.

Consider the primary fixtures in your kitchen. Perhaps they are the refrigerator, stove, and sink (the basic elements of the classic work triangle). Perhaps they also include a microwave, a separate cooktop, or some other appliance. For maximum usability, each fixture needs accessible counter space. And ideally, because it's irritating to keep bumping into people while you're cooking, any traffic in the kitchen should flow *outside* the perimeter of the primary-fixture work space (whether it forms a triangle or otherwise).

Keep in mind that the two primary fixtures people most often need to access, even if they are not involved in the cooking, are the refrigerator and sink. If possible, locate these two fixtures toward the outside edges of the work space so that people can get to them without venturing too far into the cook's domain. The same holds true for the silverware drawer.

Set up the work area around each primary fixture like a station. Just as you'd keep dish soap and sponges near the sink, you'll want pots, pans, ladles, spatulas, and other stovetop tools near the cooktop. The primary prep station should have ready access to the knives, cutting boards, peelers, measuring cups, mixing bowls, seasonings, and so on. Think about the tasks you'll do at each station, and outfit each station accordingly. This maximizes usability and efficiency and minimizes time spent rummaging around.

As an example, let's take a look at my own kitchen. It's a Pullman-style kitchen, which means it runs in a straight line with a relatively narrow aisle down the middle. Against one wall are the refrigerator, prep station, and stove. The prep station is a simple countertop for cutting, chopping, and so on. Above it is a cabinet that houses seasonings, spices, and condiments. Below it are drawers that contain cutting boards, knives, spoons, vegetable peelers, spatulas, and so on — essentially those things needed to cook or prep food. Below the drawers is a cabinet that holds pots and pans.

The idea is that the food moves along an assembly line, from the refrigerator to the prep area and then to the stove. To the right of the stove is a small countertop for staging the serving of food; the cabinetry above and below this countertop houses serving bowls, serving plates, and so on. Under-counter drawers here store eating utensils, serving spoons, and so on.

Directly across the center aisle from the prep station is the sink. Next to the sink is another prep station with a cutting board, food processor, and large stand mixer. This station is dedicated to any food prep that would involve the sink or baking. Again, there are cabinets and drawers above and below the prep station.

This is a very efficient and compact kitchen layout. And the kitchen is open to the living area, so that the cook can stand at the stove and socialize with people in the living area.

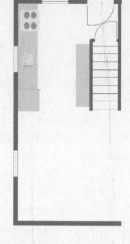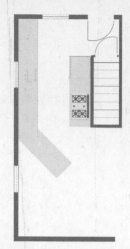

THE FLOOR PLAN: The original Pullman-style kitchen was cramped and hard to work in. The refrigerator, sink, and stove were grouped on one side, with an open countertop on the opposite side. Moving the fridge and stove to the opposite side gave each appliance adequate counter space and created prep stations. With this new setup, cooking is efficient and enjoyable.

Original floor plan

Renovated floor plan

EXTERIOR WALL: The renovated kitchen features a long expanse of open countertop for food preparation, along with a table that angles out from the wall, allowing diners to sit at both sides without obstructing traffic.

TOP FIVE KITCHEN DESIGN PRINCIPLES

1. Identify primary fixtures.

2. Locate primary fixtures near each other.

3. Assign counter space to each primary fixture.

4. Identify workstations and set them up with the appropriate tools.

5. Direct traffic flow outside the perimeter of workstations.

INTERIOR WALL: On the inside wall, the stove is flanked by more countertops, with cabinetry above and below housing all the necessary tools for stovetop cooking.

BATHROOM DESIGN

The size and luxury quotient of the bathroom should depend on the priorities of the homeowner. You may want a deluxe bathroom with a spa, rain shower, and double sinks, or you may decide upon a more utilitarian setup with a compact shower, sink, and toilet. You may want two bathrooms, or even three. If you have young children, you may want a tub. If your family spends a lot of time playing or working outdoors, you may want a half bath near the main entrance, so you can wash up easily without tracking in dirt. A micro powder room as part of a mudroom would be a great convenience.

Regardless of your particular priorities, know that you can have a well-appointed bathroom in a very modest footprint. The fast-paced evolution of design for RVs, apartments, and other small living spaces has led to some-times radical innovation in the bathroom. You can find wall-hung toilets that extend as little as 20 inches from the wall, and sinks that extend as little as 11 inches. Toilet manufacturers are even beginning to make integrated toilet-sink combinations, which are very compact and environmentally friendly to boot, since they use the wastewater from the sink to fill and flush the toilet. In some incredibly compact models, the sink replaces the lid of the toilet's flush tank. With these compact fixtures, you can convert a space as small as 12 square feet into a half bathroom. That means you could house the bathroom in the space under the stairs or in a small closet. (But note that local building codes vary in terms of how much space they require to be allotted to bathroom fixtures; you'll want to check with your local building department before you begin to do any real design work.)

Of course, size isn't the only consideration of bathroom design. Ergonomics and style are again the primary guiding principles. Above all else, a bathroom should be easy to use, comfortable, and inviting.

Sometimes it helps to look outside the common expectation to see what other cultures consider to be good ergonomics and style. Take, for example, the Japanese conception of the bathroom. Here in the West we think of a bath-tub as something to get clean in. In Japan a tub is for soaking, and you clean yourself before you enter the tub. We place the tub (or shower), the toilet, and the sink in the same room. This setup would be unthinkable in a traditional Japanese bathroom; there, each of the bathroom fixtures would have its own alcove or room. The tub, which would be a soaking tub, would be in a separate area from the toilet, and the sink would be in yet another space. The bathroom would also include a "scrubbing" station, usually a low stool with a shower wand close by: you sit on the stool, scrub yourself with a loofa sponge or scrub brush, and use the handheld shower wand for rinsing. Only after a thorough scrub would you use the soaking tub. The bathroom floors and walls would be tiled with floor drains. Since everyone using the tub is already clean, several family members might use the same water. This would save on both water and the energy to heat it.

The Japanese setup might seem byzantine, but let's examine it in light of a small house with only one bathroom. The space where you enter the bathroom houses the sink. (This area could also house a stackable washer and dryer.) A door on one side leads to the tub, and a door on the other side to the toilet.

Using fixtures designed for small spaces, such as a wall-hung toilet and slim-profile sink, a bathroom can be fit under a staircase or in a space the size of a closet. This micro powder room offers all the amenities of a half bathroom, in half the space.

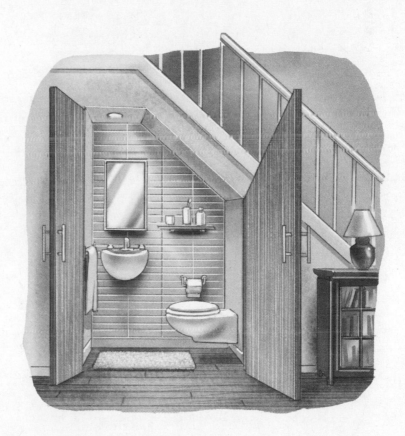

I think this seems like a very practical idea, and a good way to extend the use of a single bathroom. Someone could soak in the tub undisturbed, even if someone else needed to use the toilet. Anyone wanting to wash his or her hands could do so without disturbing either the person in the tub or the person using the toilet. With an exhaust fan in the toilet room, a particular social anxiety about using a toilet in the same space as other people could be eliminated.

For sheer convenience, I would recommend a Japanese-style bathroom for at least one of the bathrooms in any home. It's the epitome of ergonomic design, merging functionality with comfort to enhance the experience of the user.

10 WAYS TO MAKE A BATHROOM MARVELOUS

1. Natural materials

2. Radiant floor heat (your feet will appreciate it)

3. Rain shower (whether a head or freestanding over the tub)

4. Shower stool (lets you sit under your rain shower)

5. Spa or deep soaking tub

6. Tub caddy (portable shelf to hold reading materials, candles, and so on while you're soaking)

7. Heated towel rack

8. Bidet or heated toilet seat

9. Sound system (good music adds to the soothing atmosphere)

10. Mood lighting (a dimmer switch on the lights, or somewhere to set a candle)

Japanese-Style Bathroom Layouts

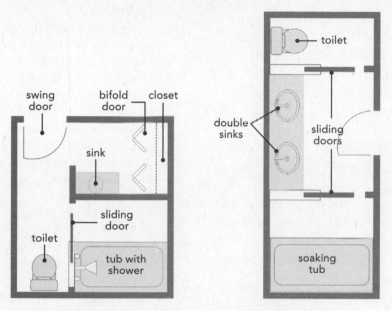

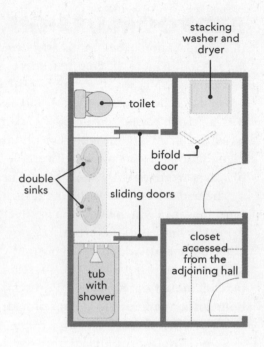

Like any bathroom, a Japanese-style bathroom can be configured in many different ways. The main point is that the toilet, bathtub, and sink are each in their own space. Entry to each space is usually guarded by a sliding door, for the simple convenience of saving space.

A Japanese-style soaking tub is usually small, deep, and square. It's a real luxury in any bathroom.

BEDROOM DESIGN

In a compact home, bedrooms are normally modest in size, leaving most of the home's footprint to the common spaces such as the living room, dining area, and kitchen. "Modest" does not have to negate the possibility of elegance and ergonomics, however. Many of the plans in this book call for a master bedroom with a private bathroom, a modern luxury that is especially appreciated by parents sharing a home with their children. And all of the plans strive for an ergonomic bedroom layout, with ample closet space, good traffic flow, and furnishings arranged with an eye toward usability and style.

The bed is likely to be the main furnishing in any bedroom, and which type goes into which bedroom (or sleeping area) will depend on who will be using the bed, and how often, and how much of the floor space you wish to allot to the bed. A couple will normally prefer a full- or queen-size bed. (A king-size bed is not out of the question, even in a compact home, but it does take up more floor space.) Children may find great delight in a bunk bed. A home office can double as a guest bedroom with a small sofa that converts to a bed when visitors arrive.

Some of the more unusual, space-saving bed designs include the following:

Murphy-style beds. Murphy beds (page 134) fold up into a wall cabinet of some type, effectively concealing themselves when not in use. They first came into vogue in urban apartments in the 1920s and '30s. Today they are making a comeback, and they are available in a number of configurations. They can be designed to fold up either from the end or from the side. Some are part of a wall unit that can include dresser or nightstand space. You can even find bunk beds in the Murphy fold-up style.

Suspended beds. Some manufacturers are now promoting a bed engineered to be suspended from the ceiling and raised and lowered electronically. In the raised position the bed resembles a shallow rectangular box attached to the ceiling. In the lowered position it appears to be a conventional bed, without a bed frame, resting on the floor. This is a great alternative to the Murphy bed if you have high ceilings.

Trundle beds and daybeds. A trundle bed is defined as a single bed that is housed beneath another bed. The trundle bed is simply pulled out when it's needed, either to be used on its own as a single bed or to convert the overhead bed into a double bed. This style of bed is ideal for a child's room (sleepovers,

Advances in Pullouts

If you don't want to allot any of your home's footprint to guest quarters, you might think about investing in pullout sofas for your living room. Pullouts have long had a bad reputation for being uncomfortable beds, giving rise to backaches and crabby mornings. But over the past decade or so there have been significant advances in the design of the bedding portion of these sofas. Today they are nearly as comfortable as conventional bedding. Three of the sofas in my house are pullout sofas; this means I can accommodate an additional six people if necessary.

anyone?) or in a guest room. It also works well in a home office, with an overhead daybed. With large throw pillows, the daybed affords a private sofalike space for reading and relaxing, and the trundle bed allows the office to double as a guest room that can accommodate two people.

Pullman-style beds. Another bedding innovation that applies itself nicely to small houses is the Pullman-style convertible bed, which was made in numerous variations by the Pullman Company for railway sleeping cars around the world. During the day, passengers could sit on a built-in couch. At night, they could pull up and latch the seat back into a horizontal position over the seat cushion, making a bunk bed. There are versions of the classic Pullman bunk bed available today (they're especially popular on cruise ships), but you can find convertible beds in all shapes, sizes, and configurations. Many convert from seating to beds, but others begin with anything from desks to shelving that convert to beds (page 135).

A platform bed can provide multifaceted storage for a compact bedroom. Clothing or other belongings can be kept in drawers beneath the bed, while the overhead shelf is the perfect spot for clocks, cell-phone chargers, and reading material, and it can be fitted with reading lights beneath. (For more built-in storage options, see page 139.)

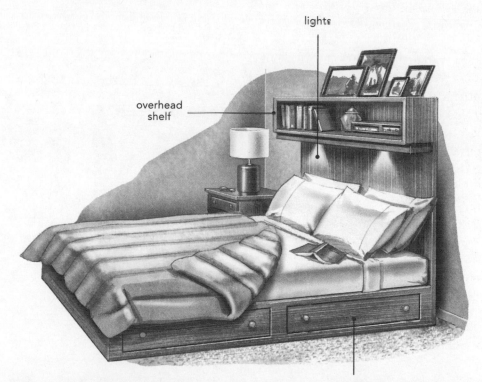

lights

overhead shelf

Platform bed with bookshelf headboard

storage drawers

Murphy-Style Beds

A traditional Murphy-style bed folds up into a wall cabinet. When unfolded, the cabinet "headboard" may house shelves, lights, or any number of other fixtures.

Unfolded: the bed

Folded up: a wall cabinet

Even bunk beds are available in the fold-up, Murphy-bed style, and they make great sleeping quarters for visiting kids.

Unfolded: bunk beds

Folded up: a wall cabinet

Convertible Beds

Unfolded: a twin bed

Folded up: a desk

Some styles of fold-up beds convert from beds to desks or tables. They're popular in studio apartments, and they work well in a home office that doubles as a guest room.

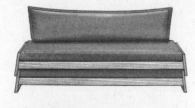

Stacked, with cushion: a daybed

Modern furniture manufacturers are producing a wide range of convertible beds, such as a stacking version that converts from a couch to a single bed to a double bed.

Stacked, without cushion: a twin bed

Unstacked: a double bed

DINING AREA DESIGN

In a compact house, the dining area is often integrated with, or open to, the kitchen to maximize usability while minimizing footprint. As with the dining area in any size home, a sideboard or hutch is helpful for housing utensils, serving dishes, napkins, and the like — and storing these items in the dining area leaves room for storage of pots, pans, and other cookware in the kitchen. But of primary importance, of course, is the table.

In general, it makes sense to size the dining table for the number of people who will usually be eating at it, but to be able to expand the size of the table to accommodate guests. You might consider a drop-leaf table, with a leaf (or leaves) that folds down against the legs. Or you may prefer an extension table, with removable leaves that can be stored in a closet when they're not in use. Folding tables are another good option, and we're not talking here about flimsy card tables that rock like an earthquake when you lean your elbows upon them. You can find sturdy, stylish, modern folding tables from most furniture manufacturers. Some even fold up into chic cabinets that you can hang on the wall in the dining area — the perfect storage solution!

When you do expand your dining table to accommodate guests, they'll need chairs to sit in. Like folding tables, folding chairs have come a long way since their card-table days. These are not your grandmother's folding chairs. Today you can find them in a variety of styles, colors, materials, and finishes. Many are meant for everyday use, not occasional use, so they're sturdy, comfortable, and stylish. The fact that they fold up is simply a feature that makes them portable.

I once lived in a house with a small second-floor porch. It was a nice spot for reading, up and away from the noise of the street. It also faced east and had beautiful morning light, and I wanted to set it up as a space for weekend breakfasts, but without crowding the porch with furniture. So I set up the porch with patio-style cushioned chairs for reading and relaxing. I then invested in a table and chair set: a double drop-leaf table and four folding chairs that could be stored beneath the table when the leaves were dropped. A shallow drawer under the tabletop could be used to store placemats and utensils. The table was on casters and could be rolled to the side, to function as a side table, when not in use. We would start with breakfast at the table and graduate to the cushioned chairs to read the Sunday paper — elegance and functionality, all in a compact space.

The Modern Folding Table

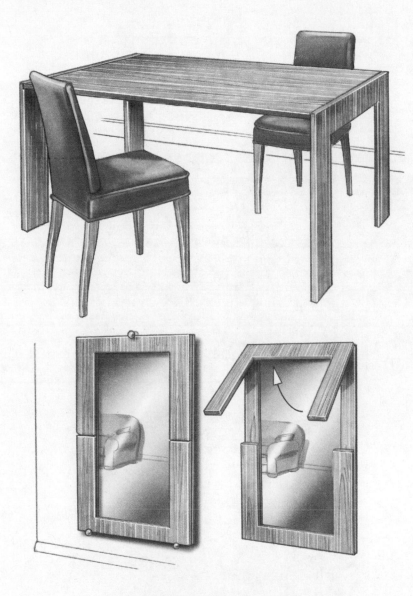

If you occasionally need extra table space, look to the modern folding table, which is portable, sturdy, and compact in storage. Some versions even fold up into a wall-hung unit; the underside of the table could house a mirror, and the frame unfolds to become the table legs.

A wall-hung unit: the frame unfolds to become the table's legs.

The Modern Drop-Leaf Table

A modernist drop-leaf table is flexible and stylish. With both leaves extended, it serves as a full-size dining table. With one leaf dropped, it's a small table or desk. You could even drop both leaves and set it against the wall as a console table.

STORAGE: BUILT-INS AND CLOSETS

Whether you're building new or renovating an existing house, storage in a compact home is a high design priority. A cluttered home is neither comfortable nor inviting. We must have space for storing our belongings, and in a compact home the storage solutions often must be clever. The designer must look at every inch of space within the home, from the roof down to the foundation, with an eye toward creating accessible, useful storage.

Here is where built-ins can be useful. A house normally holds a surprising amount of unused space. In a well-designed compact home, that space is put to use for storage. The space under a stairwell can become a closet and/or an array of drawers or shelves. In bungalows and cottages, where a low roofline creates sloping ceilings on the second floor, the eaves space — between the outer wall of the second-floor rooms and the exterior wall of the building — can house drawers or cabinets. In any room, for that matter, built-in drawers, cabinets, or shelves are excellent ways to increase storage; narrow shelves can even be seated between studs, which gains a bit of storage space without subtracting it from the footprint of the room. A bedroom built-in storage unit might combine features, with drawers near floor level, a clothes-hanging rod at eye level, and a storage locker above, extending right up to the ceiling.

Speaking of cabinets extending up to the ceiling, in traditional kitchen design the cabinets usually do not extend any higher than the average cook can reach, leaving a wide gap between the top of the cabinets and the ceiling. That wasted space can be reclaimed easily by designing cabinets that extend all the way up to the ceiling, or by installing a custom-built set of storage cabinets above the regular kitchen cabinets. Use this upper-level space to contain the tools, serving ware, utensils, and other kitchen gear that you don't use very often. With a step stool stored nearby, you'll have ready access to those items whenever you need them, and by utilizing this normally forgotten space you can increase your kitchen storage by about 20 percent.

You can increase bedroom storage similarly by installing cabinets or drawers beneath bed frames. For most people this space is simply a staging ground for dust bunnies, but it's ideal for storing out-of-season clothing and extra linens. Finished wood drawers are handsome, but a few plastic storage tubs work just as well. I use under-bed storage tubs to store extra sheets and blankets. And at the head of the bed, consider installing a shelf for books, a reading lamp, a clock, your cell phone, and whatever else you like to keep at your

Stairs Storage Solutions

A clever carpenter can reconfigure the underside of each stair step to be a sliding drawer, with a small tab pull on one side. The drawers will be relatively shallow, but there will be a whole staircase of them!

Another way to utilize the underside of stairs for storage is to build cabinets below, whether open or with doors. These cabinets will be deep and irregularly shaped; they can add a funky modern vibe to any living space.

Pull-out drawers fit prettily beneath a staircase, with angled edges to parallel the rise of the steps. The Shakers would approve of the economy and utilization of otherwise wasted space.

Between-Stud Recessed Shelving

The shallow, narrow cabinets that can be built between studs, recessed into the wall, make excellent pantry storage in a compact kitchen.

Between-stud shelving is also a good option for storing decorative items in a hallway. If you plan for the cabinets during the construction of your home, you can even arrange to have them wired with interior lighting, to lend a museum-like ambience to their contents.

Under-Eaves Storage

Many small homes, and especially Capes and bungalows, have slanted ceilings in second-floor bedrooms, due to the pitch of a low-slung roof. Built-in drawers, extending into the under-eaves space, are a traditional way to utilize the otherwise wasted under-eaves space.

A bathroom with a sloping ceiling offers an opportunity for built-in storage, and with a skylight set above, it becomes an ideal greenhouse spot, flooding the bathroom with natural light while maintaining privacy from neighbors. If the skylight is operable — that is, it can be opened — it will aid in ventilation as well.

Under-Eaves Nooks

Another clever use of the under-eaves space is built-in bunks, with between-stud recessed shelving at the head of the bed and under-bed drawers. This is a pretty little arrangement for a child's room or a guest room, with the bunk nooks offering a feeling of coziness and privacy.

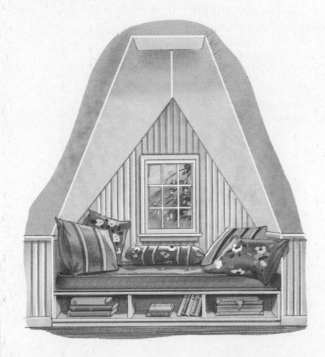

An elegant, interesting home makes the best use of its space while also offering private nooks for reading, relaxing, or just getting away from the chaos of family. A window seat is just such a getaway, and because it makes good use of otherwise wasted space, it's an ideal element of a compact home design.

bedside (page 134). In fact, you could fashion an entire bookshelf headboard, a unique and useful addition to your bedroom decor.

A window seat is an old idea that warrants reviving. Set beneath a wide, often decorative window, with a cushion on its surface, a window seat usually looks quite elegant. And with drawers or a cabinet fitted beneath it, it's useful storage, too. It's an ideal spot to sit and read, and it's also an excellent place to store seasonal bedding, toys, and games.

Of course, the traditional storage space — the closet — remains a fixture for the compact home. If you're renovating an existing older home, such as a condominium in an older Victorian house, you may find that the closets are tiny, if, indeed, there are closets at all! In these cases especially, organization is key. In recent years closet organization has become an art and a science, and a profitable business for many. A number of companies now offer excellent closet organization tools and design services, but you can plan and install your own closet organization system for a fraction of the cost. To begin, consider what you'll be storing in the closet and how it can best be assigned to use all the space, from floor to ceiling. Then consider ergonomics. Using every inch of closet space for storage is not very helpful if you can't identify or access your things when you want them. For myself, I tend to use shelving that has built-in clothes-hanging rails and a lot of clear plastic storage tubs. You may prefer a wall of shoe racks

OFF-SEASON STORAGE

One way to use small closets efficiently is to think seasonally. I have some very heavy winter clothing that I wear when I plow my driveway, snowshoe, or cross-country ski. Where I live this clothing is only necessary from mid-December through mid-March each year. For the other nine months of the year, I need to store this gear. Here is where clear storage tubs come in handy. I fold up and store this deep-winter clothing and equipment in tubs in the back of a closet, and I exchange them for tubs holding shorts and bathing suits when the snow begins to fall. Plastic tubs are pretty low-tech and not for the chic at heart, but they do work well. You also could use something as simple as zippered plastic clothing bags or as fancy as cedar closets.

The same idea holds true for all other seasonal items. Storing out-of-season gear, from clothes to outdoor furniture, lawn mowers, snowblowers, and so on, not only saves space but protects those items (provided you store them correctly) from the weather, insects and mice, and other factors encouraged by neglect.

and shelves with woven cotton baskets; a child may do best with a low rack of clothes-hanging hooks and deep open shelves, with the higher spaces saved for clothes to grow into or extra bedding. The point is to design the closet for the user. If your inclinations or needs change over time, well, reorganizing the closet is always an interesting endeavor — and just one more opportunity to purge the excess and simplify your life.

POCKET AND SLIDING DOORS

Like the window seat, the pocket door is an architectural element you don't see much anymore. In early American architecture it was traditionally used between the parlor and the dining room, where it could be opened or closed depending on the needs of the family. After a good meal the family and guests could retire to the parlor for coffee, brandy, or dessert and close the pocket doors to the dining room to hide the mess. (In more aristocratic households, this is when the servants would come in to clean up.)

Because pocket doors and other types of sliding doors don't have a swing radius, they take up little space, which makes them ideal for compact houses. In fact, you'll see them in use in many of the designs in this book. A sliding door is excellent between children's bedrooms. It can be opened on a rainy day to turn small bedrooms into a large playroom. And it can add to the magic of pretend play, as it can be the curtain of a star-studded theatrical thriller or the Black Gate of Mordor.

DECKS, PORCHES, AND PATIOS

One traditional way to extend a home's living space is to add a deck, porch, or patio. With the addition of a range of amenities — a table and chairs, lounge furniture, a bar, a grill, an outdoor kitchen, a pizza oven, a fire pit, a fireplace — these outdoor spaces beckon inhabitants outside to enjoy the open air. They make a home seem more welcoming, more spacious, and better integrated with the outdoor environment. (Pergolas and gazebos can serve in the same way.)

Decks, porches, and patios can be part of a budgeted building program. They can be built to function as an outdoor living space at the onset and, when finances allow, later enclosed, insulated, and wired for electricity. In the same way, an open porch can be destined for conversion to a sunporch or screened porch when time and finances allow. Of course, if this kind of expansion is part of the overall house design, then consideration for its final use should be given from the very beginning. For example, if you intend to eventually enclose a patio, you may want to lay the foundation for the eventual enclosure at the outset, so you don't have to dig up the patio later to put down a foundation with adequate structural support. You may want to embed radiant-heat tubing in the patio floor, with the intent to connect the tubing to the house's heating system when the patio is enclosed. If you intend to someday enclose a deck, you'll want to consider how its roofline will intersect with the roofline of the existing house. If you intend to someday enclose a porch, insulating the porch floor will be much easier during construction, rather than retrofitting the floor with insulation.

A sunporch doubles as an elegant open-to-the-outdoors living space and an energy-saving design component. Usually a sunporch is an enclosed, insulated porch with large arrays of windows or glass panels and some type of masonry floor. When oriented correctly — generally to the south of the home — it can function as a passive solar collector, with the masonry floor absorbing the warmth of the sun during the day and radiating that heat back into the home during the night. (A thermostatically controlled duct blower can assist with moving warm air from the porch into the rest of the house.) Of course, provisions must be made for adequate ventilation during the warmer months of the year; operable windows and skylights can help with this, as can deciduous trees, whose leaves block the summer sunlight. Curtains made from greenhouse-grade shade fabrics can also help. These fabrics are usually made from knitted polypropylene yarn and are graded by the amount of shade they provide, from 20 to 80 percent. They are relatively inexpensive, and since they are porous they allow air to circulate and don't block the ventilation. I made a roll-up shade from an 80 percent shade fabric for one end of my own sunroom, using the hardware from an old bamboo roll-up shade. I mounted it above the windows on the west end of my sunroom, and I roll it down when the afternoon sun is a bit too strong.

LANDSCAPING SMALL SPACES

When a compact home is paired with a compact yard, you'll want to make the most of your outdoor space to optimize its functionality. The size of the yard determines how much space you can allot to any particular landscape design item. Big decks mean less space for trees and shrubs. This is not necessarily bad; a big deck offers more outdoor living space and reduces the yard area that needs to be tended. Again ergonomics become important. If you are not a gardener and like to entertain outdoors in the summer, a big deck is a good idea for you. On the other hand, if you love to garden and your kids like playing outside, then you'll want to maximize the open space in your yard. Good landscape design, like all home design, is driven by the intended use of the space. Figure out how you'll use the yard, and you'll be well on your way toward designing it.

If you live in a suburban setting, privacy may be an issue for your outdoor living spaces. Again, figure out how you'll use the yard, and then examine how the landscaping offers privacy for each of the spaces you'll use. Where privacy is lacking, you can add living fences (shrubs and the like), wood or PVC fencing, screens, or roll-down blinds. Such features not only enhance the functionality of the outdoor space but also add equity to the property.

SEVEN TIPS FOR ECOFRIENDLY LANDSCAPING

1. Use native plants, shrubs, trees, grasses, and flowers whenever possible.

2. Plant less grass and more shrubs and trees. The ideal is not to have to own a mower.

3. Reuse and repurpose materials whenever possible. This includes whatever material exists on your property when you begin construction.

4. During construction, preserve existing shrubs and trees as much as possible. A lot of natural energy went into growing them.

5. Choose low-maintenance plants.

6. Recycle rainwater for irrigation.

7. Value your soils. Landscape to avoid soil erosion, and fertilize your soil with compost rather than chemicals. A healthy soil will foster healthy landscaping.

CHAPTER 3

ENERGY: EFFICIENCY AND SUSTAINABILITY

ONE OF THE GREATEST ADVANTAGES OF A COMPACT HOUSE IS THE FACT THAT IT IS EASIER TO BUILD (OR RETROFIT) GREEN. OF COURSE, ENERGY EFFICIENCY AND SUSTAINABILITY MEASURES MAKE SENSE FOR EVERY HOME, BUT BECAUSE OF THEIR SMALL SIZE, COMPACT HOMES HAVE A SMALLER ENVIRONMENTAL IMPACT AND OFFER THE POTENTIAL FOR VAST ENERGY SAVINGS.

Energy efficiency has become a critical issue in house design. An ever-larger percentage of the household budget is devoted to energy: heating, cooling, hot water, and power. As you might expect, technology in the field is morphing quickly to meet the needs and demands of the marketplace. Whether you're building new or retrofitting, options abound.

We'll review some of the more common energy-efficiency and sustainability measures here, but keep in mind that this is a rapidly expanding field where design and technology are constantly reinventing themselves. That said, when you're investigating the innovative ideas and technology of the marketplace, be sure that ergonomics and style reign as your guiding principles (as discussed in chapter 2). No innovation, regardless of how amazing it is, is worth the money if it doesn't actually improve upon the enjoyment of your home.

CHOOSING APPROPRIATE TECHNOLOGY

The term *appropriate technology* is usually applied in connection with discussions of what's "right" for third-world countries. It is my position that this concept can — and should — be extended to the modern Western world as well. The technology we *need* is only that which improves the functioning of our lives. It is, in a way, psychological ergonomics: choosing technology that makes the human experience more comfortable and engaging, *not* technology that makes our lives more disengaged, clamorous, or stressful.

The appropriateness of technology lies in the eye of the beholder. I need a high-end computer with a high-speed Internet connection to be able to work with graphics and engineering programs. But I have the simplest cell phone available; I just don't need it that much. On the other hand, I have a friend who travels the world for her employer. She has a sophisticated cell phone with international capabilities and a simple tablet computer; that's what she needs. We don't have the most technologically advanced gear in every category; we have what is *appropriate* for each of us.

The challenge is not to go down the technology buffet line and load our plates with more than we can manage just because it's there; that's wasteful. The challenge is to be mindful of what we buy and how it impacts us and the world. We need only what allows us to live and work comfortably. Anything more is excessive.

The selection of technologies that are appropriate for the modern home should be driven by a number of factors:

▶ **Available resources.** Most technologies need suppliers, support, energy sources, and so on. For example, photovoltaics is a powerful up-and-coming green technology, but most homeowners will need regional infrastructure (suppliers, local service and repair) to implement it successfully in their homes.

▶ **The needs of the user.** Consider current and future needs. The big question is, what do I *really* need? And the next: what will I need in 5, 10, or 20 years? You don't want to invest in more technology than you need, but at the same time, you want to design your house to be able to adapt easily to future needs.

▶ **Budget.** How much technology is too much from a cost standpoint?

▶ **Obsolescence.** The longer appliances and equipment last, the cheaper they are to own. Then again, these days most electronics equipment and quite a bit of the sustainable-energy technology is reinventing itself at an ever faster pace, so that the equipment you buy today may be old hat within a year. Older technologies generally work fine — consider the number of post-and-beam houses going up even today — but you'll need to weigh carefully the worth of making any significant investments in "new" technology that is likely to be in its second- or third-generation iteration by the time you actually finish building your home.

BUILDING HOME-ENERGY SAVINGS

Houses that prioritize energy efficiency and sustainability can be described by the degree of independence they enjoy from the power grid and outside energy sources. These are not hard-and-fast definitions but various steps along a continuum, from traditional dependence on the power grid and public infrastructure at one end to complete independence on the other.

▶ **Ultra-low-energy building:** A building that just "sips" power from the national grid. It may produce most of its own power and makes great use of energy-efficient and sustainable architecture, materials, and appliances.

▶ **Zero-energy building:** A building with zero net energy consumption and producing zero net carbon emissions. The ideal house of this type would be energy independent, producing all of the energy it consumed itself. It would use sustainable-energy sources such as passive solar design and wind for its power, thereby producing no carbon emissions.

▶ **Energy-plus building:** A building that produces more power than it uses. In such a case, a homeowner may be able to sell the excess power to the national grid.

▶ **Autonomous building:** Independent from infrastructural support, or totally off the grid: no public electricity, gas, fuel oil, water, or sewage. This type of house is completely self-reliant.

To approach or achieve energy independence, these homes rely on sustainable architecture and design, renewable energy sources (wind power, passive solar, photovoltaics, wood burning, and so on), highly efficient appliances and fixtures, and energy-efficient landscaping. Some homeowners set out to build an off-the-grid autonomous building from the start. Many more begin with an ultra-low-energy building and over time upgrade their energy infrastructure and efficiency until they become autonomous. Passive systems become active; power storage capacity is added; new systems are introduced over time. The growth from simple to complex usually proceeds one step at a time — it's manageable, understandable, and cost-effective for homeowners in all income brackets.

GREEN ARCHITECTURE AND DESIGN

I consider building green, as ecologically conscious architecture and design is commonly known, to be part of a big-picture approach to ergonomics. The green movement is the ergonomics of the environment. It aspires to the same goals as ergonomics: the comfort and betterment of living for humans. It strives to balance the needs of humans with the needs of sustaining a healthy environment. In general, it prioritizes the following factors:

▶ **Local conditions.** There is no perfect combination of technologies that will make a building green. The right combination is one that works the best and is the most ecologically efficient for a particular building on a particular site. Green architecture in the American Southwest is very different than in New England.

▶ **Local materials.** Using local materials reduces the costs and pollution associated with transportation and stimulates the local economy. It can also help stylistically, tying a home in with the local environment. I live in an area where roofing slate, red-clay brick, and cement are produced from local materials; green buildings in my area make great use of these materials, and as a result a local architectural aesthetic is rising up, establishing stylistic relationships among homes in the area.

▶ **Sustainable or low-impact materials.** Green architects and builders give a lot of weight to using sustainable and low-emission materials, for the health of the landscape and the occupants of the home.

▶ **Minimal impact on the landscape.** Construction disturbs the environment of the building lot. With some forethought and planning with your construction team (especially the excavator), you can minimize negative impacts and in some cases even improve the landscape (for example, by regrading to minimize soil erosion).

▶ **Proper siting.** In contrast to suburban developments of yore, where houses were aligned on a preordained network of streets, modern green architects aim for optimal siting, taking into account factors such as sun exposure, passive solar gain, privacy, water runoff and drainage, and integration with the landscape.

▶ **Energy-efficient appliances and systems.** Green architecture seeks to limit the carbon footprint of a building and its consumption of carbon-based fuels. Green architects are calling for low-flush toilets, low-flow faucets, rainwater catchment systems, gray-water recycling systems, Energy Star–rated (or better) appliances, electrical outlet shutoffs to minimize ghost loads (the electricity appliances consume even when they are turned off), and recycling infrastructure (which can be as simple as allotting space in the home specifically for recycling bins), among other measures.

▶ **Alternative energy systems.** Green architecture often incorporates alternative energy sources. Again, local conditions dictate the choice of energy sources. Solar heating may not be nearly as practical in New England as in the Southwest. Then again, wood for wood-burning stoves is more available in New England than in the Southwest. The area I live in is just south of the anthracite coal region of Pennsylvania; this makes coal a contender for heating.

LEED CERTIFICATION

Some green buildings obtain certification of their "green-ness" through the LEED (Leadership in Energy and Environmental Design) program. The LEED Green Building Rating System is a program developed and administered by the nonprofit U.S. Green Building Council. LEED buildings are rated based on five categories:

▶ Sustainable site development

▶ Water efficiency

▶ Energy efficiency and ecofriendliness

▶ Materials selection

▶ Indoor environmental quality

The U.S. Green Building Council rates buildings by their degree of compliance with the values of the council. Buildings can be rated silver, gold, or platinum, with platinum obviously the best. If you're interested in pursuing LEED certification, seek out the website of the U.S. Green Building Council, which carries full details on the program.

▶ **Innovative design.** Green architecture has championed new technologies like solar, green roofs, and geothermal heating and cooling. Green architecture also embraces older, proven design ideas: the use of thermal masses, siting structures to take advantage of natural elements and landscaping, landscaping with ecofriendly native plants, minimizing water use and maximizing water recycling, and more. Good green design draws from the best of what design has to offer in order to accomplish its goals.

INSULATION

It can't be emphasized enough: superior insulation is *key* to energy efficiency, not to mention reducing your energy bills. If you're building a new home, you can plan for insulation from the start and make use of the best technology and materials currently available. If you're retrofitting, your options may be limited by the structure and systems of your home, but be assured that having adequate insulation will make a world of difference in terms of both your comfort level and your energy budget.

Insulation is all about the outer shell of the house. It entails not just thickening this shell to better hold (or repel) heat (or cold) but also stopping air infiltration through the use of well-sealed windows and doors, house wraps, caulks and other sealants, and so on.

As the house becomes tighter (better sealed), ventilation becomes a concern. In a well-insulated house, air-handling systems are used to bring in fresh air. These systems will be equipped with heat/cool transfer mechanisms. All of these advances will translate into more expensive construction costs, but they will quickly pay off with equal or greater energy savings.

NATURAL COOLING

If you live in southern climates, keeping the house cool is a primary concern, but even in northern ranges cooling is important for summer months. Air-conditioning has become the default mechanism by which we cool our houses, but it's a tremendous energy hog. There are many ways to cool a house naturally and either avoid or minimize the use of air-conditioning:

▶ **Shade trees.** Deciduous trees planted on the south side of a house afford shade to the house in the summer. The leaves drop in autumn, allowing some solar heating of the house through winter.

▶ **Deep porches.** These keep the sun off the lower part of a house and also allow the windows to be open for ventilation even in wet weather.

▶ **Deep roof overhangs.** They shade windows from the overhead sun in summer while still allowing the lower-angled sun of winter to shine in. Like deep porches, deep roof overhangs also allow windows to remain open in wet weather. An added benefit is that the overhang protects windows from dust so they don't need to be cleaned as often.

▶ **Window awnings.** Awnings keep solar heat out during the summer months. Normally they are fabricated from either sheet metal or canvas.

▶ **Insulation.** Well-insulated exterior walls and ceilings, even in the attic, keep the summer heat from penetrating into the living space.

▶ **Attic ventilation.** As warm air rises from the house and the sun beats down on the roof, temperatures in the attic can become stifling. Eventually some of that heat finds its way down into the living space. With soffit and ridge vents, or with an attic exhaust fan operating on a thermostat, you can exhaust that heat and keep the house cooler.

▶ **Double-hung windows.** Tall double-hung windows that can open from both the top and the bottom draw in cool air from below and vent warm air at the top. Double-hung windows in older homes were designed around this type of natural ventilation. Of course, full-length window screens are a necessity.

▶ **Clerestory windows.** A clerestory is a series of operable windows situated just below the ceiling line of a room or house. When opened they allow warm air out and draw cool air into the living space below. They also allow natural light into the core of a house. Clerestory lighting and ventilation have been in use since the Middle Ages.

▶ **Cross-ventilation.** Windows and doors positioned across from each other allow for cross-ventilation.

▶ **Stack ventilation.** Stack ventilation takes advantage of the natural buoyancy of warm air by creating a passageway through which that warm air can rise, venting the warm air toward the top of the building and thus drawing in cooler air from below.

Clerestory Windows

View from the outside

Clerestory windows sit just under the roofline, allowing natural light into the core of a home while maintaining privacy. They also enhance natural ventilation by pulling up and releasing warm air from the core of the building, which in turn draws in cooler air from below.

View from the inside

▶ **Light colors.** Light colors reflect light. So, light-colored roofing and siding reflect sunlight and, therefore, most of the heat generated when a building absorbs sunlight.

▶ **Shutters and insulated shades.** Operable shutters can be closed during the day to keep out sunlight and solar gain. Insulated shades can be used to keep the sun out in the summertime and to keep the heat in during winter months.

▶ **Thermal mass.** Massive (usually masonry) exterior walls absorb heat during the day and release it slowly, usually overnight. The time lag between exposure to the sun and when the heat finally penetrates into the living space works to the homeowner's advantage, particularly when paired with ventilation mechanisms. This is an ancient and time-honored building technique. Adobe structures of the American Southwest operate on this principle.

▶ **High ceilings.** The larger the interior air mass in a room, the longer it will take to heat up. (This is an advantage in warmer climates, but in colder climates that same air mass has to be heated in the winter.)

▶ **Ceiling and whole-house fans.** Fans are a cost-effective way to cool interior space, whether individual fans in rooms or a whole-house fan located centrally. Even with air-conditioning, moving air can make it feel cooler inside. This allows the thermostat to be turned up a few degrees.

▶ **Evaporative or swamp coolers.** These types of coolers work by spraying water into a fan-generated airstream. The water is released as extremely small droplets and evaporates immediately, absorbing heat. Swamp coolers can lower the temperature by as much as 20 degrees. The problem is that this kind of system also raises the humidity. In a dry climate or in an outdoor space like a deck or patio this works well and is cost-effective. I installed a swamp cooler in my greenhouse set on a thermostat to operate at 80°F (27°C). It can drop the greenhouse temperature in about 30 minutes, and the plants appreciate the extra humidity.

HOME HEATING

Most homes are heated with a central furnace of some type, and having some form of central heating makes sense. It is easy to use and maintain, works even when you're not home, and provides heat to the entire house.

With a well-insulated, well-sited compact home, however, you may find that your heating needs are minimal and can be met for the most part with some form of fuel-burning stove. The stove can either replace or augment a central heating system, depending on your needs.

There are a number of types and styles on the market. Some, such as propane heaters, are designed to heat a single room at most. Others, such as a masonry stove or woodstove, can heat an entire house, particularly if the house has an open floor plan. The type you choose will depend on a number of issues:

What are your heating needs? This question essentially asks how many BTUs (British thermal units, a measure of heating capacity) you need to do the job. If you're heating a single room, your requirements will be vastly different than if you're heating the entire house. A stove that is too large is a waste of money, and a stove that is too small won't do the job. If you're not sure about the BTUs, consult with a stove dealer, who will be able to help you figure it out.

Will the payback be worth it? Stoves can be expensive. It's important to figure the initial cost and payback time into your decision. If you intend to heat your entire home with a fuel-burning stove set in the living room, it might make sense to invest in a beautiful but expensive masonry fireplace. If you're heating a patio, a masonry heater might not be worth the cost.

How much maintenance is required? Wood-burning stoves need to be hand-fired and the ashes removed periodically. If you have a work schedule that doesn't allow you to tend one of these stoves, it may not be a good choice for you. Or you may want to use it in conjunction with a central heating system.

Home Heating Options

A simple propane- or gas-fired heater can heat an entire home, but it's most often used as a supplemental heater for an out-of-the-way room, or as a backup to a woodstove or passive solar heating system. Most units sit flat and unobtrusively against an exterior wall.

A multifuel stove is capable of burning more than one type of fuel, such as wood logs, wood pellets, coal, or even corn. It's a flexible heating option that allows homeowners to take advantage of local fuel availabilities and fluctuating prices.

A woodstove can put out a lot of heat, and in an open-concept home it may serve to heat the entire house. In wooded regions of the world, a woodstove is also a good option in terms of sustainability, as it can be fueled with local timber.

A masonry fireplace is an expensive but elegant and efficient heating option. By forcing the flue gases to pass through an extended masonry path, it absorbs every last bit of heat from a wood fire, then slowly releases that heat into the room.

HOME ENERGY SAVER

If you're thinking of purchasing and renovating a compact home rather than building a new one, the U.S. Department of Energy maintains a website that can be helpful in calculating home energy costs and the possible savings you can obtain by upgrading the home's energy systems. This site allows you to try out various models to calculate the costs and savings involved. To find the site, simply search online for "home energy saver." Once you're on the site, respond to the screens as they come up. The software powering the site will customize its responses for your location (that is, for the local climate).

Let's say you're wondering whether it makes sense to replace an oil-fired furnace with one that uses natural gas. Will it save you money? This system will calculate the savings (or not) from this change. It's a simple step to then divide the savings by the cost of the upgrade to calculate how long it would take to earn back its cost and begin real savings. With this information you can then make an educated decision about whether or not you want to make this upgrade.

Like any system, this one is imperfect. It can't account for every possible variation in home energy use. For example, if you want to install a biomass-burning stove to save on heating costs, you won't get any good advice from this system at present; it's not engineered to accommodate this option. Or let's say you live in Florida or some other Southern state where it's warm enough that you do not need whole-house central heating. But it does get cold enough in the depths of winter that sometimes you need heat for a week or so, in which case you use electric room heaters. If you were asking the system to calculate your home energy use, you would tell the system that you don't have central heat, but the system doesn't offer you a way to note that you have supplemental heaters, with concomitant increased electricity use for at least part of the winter.

But one way this system is very useful is in calculating the energy costs of a home you're considering buying. Potential energy costs should factor into any decision to purchase a home, and with this system, you can plug in the numbers for any home you are thinking about purchasing and quickly get those figures.

Supplemental Heating

Most homes have a space or two that's off the beaten path heating-wise. They may be last in line in a heating system using hot water with radiators. Or maybe they're not reached by heat from a central woodstove. Whatever the case, in certain areas of a home, such as an out-of-the-way bathroom, you may want to think about point-of-use supplemental heaters. Rather than warming up the whole house just to make the bathroom temperature tolerable or to keep its pipes from freezing, you can turn on the heat in just that room.

The most common point-of-use room heaters are small gas fireplaces or stoves, electric baseboard heaters, oil-filled radiators, and propane space heaters. In a bathroom, you might use a heated towel bar, which can provide

HVAC Storage

Heating, ventilation, and air-conditioning (HVAC) equipment is normally stored in a home's basement or attic space. In a home without a basement or attic, however, this equipment must be stored somewhere in the living space, usually in a deep closet. The house plans in this book don't generally note where the HVAC equipment should be stored, because that's a personal decision guided by a particular household's likely patterns of use. You'll want to house the equipment in whichever closet has the most space and/or is least likely to see intensive use.

enough warmth for towels and people alike. You also might consider installing an infrared heater in the bathroom ceiling. Infrared heaters warm only the surface the infrared strikes and not the room or the air in the room. This means it heats you, not the whole bathroom. Heaters like this can be installed with timer switches so they shut off in a predetermined number of minutes.

Hot Water Systems

Producing, storing, and transporting hot water is one of the greatest energy expenses in a home. In any home, sizing the water heating system to meet the expected requirements of the household is common sense. A family of three does not need the water-heating capacity of a family of six. The family of three may do fine with a hot water heater with a 40-gallon capacity. A family of six may need a hot water heater with a capacity of 90 gallons.

Then again, traditional tank-style water heaters are notoriously wasteful of energy. Holding a large amount of water at a high temperature is inefficient, even when the heater is heavily insulated. A better choice would be point-of-use water heaters that are located close to where hot water is needed and heat the water on demand. They are usually fueled by electricity or natural gas, and they are very efficient. It is the usual practice to have a unit in the kitchen, another in the bathroom, and another in the laundry. Having three separate water heaters may seem like a greater expense, but when you factor in the cost of plumbing hot water from a tank-style water heater to each point of use, along with the energy loss from the storage tank and the hot water lines, over the life of the appliance, a point-of-use system starts looking like a reasonable alternative.

ALTERNATIVE ENERGY SYSTEMS

People who want to invest in a compact home because of its lesser environmental impact and greater potential for being off the grid often are interested in alternative energy systems. Indeed, as fossil fuel prices rise, a growing population of homeowners of all types is interested in alternative energy sources, from solar hot water and solar electric to heat pumps, wind generators, and geothermal systems.

At present, alternative energy systems for homes are a big investment, even with government and municipal energy tax breaks. But as the systems become more popular, the price is beginning to come down, and free-thinking entrepreneurs are finding ways to lessen the cost with group purchasing programs, leasing programs, financing programs, and the like.

The benefit of a compact home is that its energy requirements, by sheer virtue of its lesser size, are usually less than those of a larger home. With some forethought in the design and construction phase, those requirements can be extremely low and more easily met by an alternative energy system.

There are many good books, websites, and other information sources devoted to alternative energy sources: evaluating them, choosing one for your specific needs, installing them, servicing them, payback times, and so on. If you're interested in an alternative energy system, by all means begin with some general research, but be sure to consult with local installation professionals. They'll have the experience necessary to know what types of systems work best in your region, what service and technical help is available locally, and the parameters of cost and payback time.

LANDSCAPING FOR HOME ENERGY EFFICIENCY

Landscaping specifically for the purpose of conserving energy in the home is often referred to as *energy-efficient landscaping.* An energy-efficient landscape not only can provide a beautiful, ecofriendly environment around your home but also can reduce your heating and cooling costs.

Landscaping to Cool a House

Heat from the summer sun can be absorbed through windows, the roof, and the walls of a house, leading to increased cooling requirements. You can reduce that solar heat gain by designing shade into your landscape, thus reducing your cooling costs.

The time-honored way to shade a home from summer sun is with deciduous trees planted on the south and east sides of the building (and sometimes the west side as well). When fully leafed out in the summer, they block sunlight from the home. In the winter, when their leaves have fallen, they allow sunlight through to warm the home.

A more novel method is through the use of a green roof — a rooftop with a soil base that is densely planted with hardy plants and grasses. A green roof helps cool a home by virtue of its thermal mass, much like insulation. It also works via evapotranspiration, the process by which a plant actively takes up water and releases it as vapor. Water transpired by plant leaves absorbs heat and evaporates, reducing the heat in the plant and therefore the roof.

Green roofs must be carefully designed for irrigation and drainage, structural support, and maintenance. Many green-architecture companies specialize in the construction of green roofs; you can find them with a simple search on the Internet.

Landscaping to Warm a House

The primary way to keep a home warm with landscaping is to prevent heat loss from wind. Traditional foundation plantings are one form of windbreak; though they're usually thought of as camouflage for the home's foundation, they also keep wind from hitting the foundation directly and robbing the home of heat.

If you're interested in planting a windbreak, you'll first need to know the direction of the prevailing winter wind in your microregion; generally it comes from the north or west. Then you can install plantings on that side of your home. Evergreens are the most common choice for windbreak plantings because they keep their foliage in winter. You can plant them all in a row, like a living fence, or stagger the plantings so that you can easily pass through the planting. Either setup has the same effect of breaking the force of the wind before it reaches your home.

The general recommendation is to plant windbreaks within 400 feet of your home for best effect, but not less than 100 feet from your home to allow for proper air circulation (for cooling in summer and to prevent mold and insect infestation).

Another design concept for keeping a home warm is *earth sheltering*, which positions a building to take advantage of natural landforms used as windbreaks. You might, for example, build a hillside home with its northern side embedded into the hill to take advantage of the natural windbreak and thermal mass. *Earth berming* works similarly, though in this case the landform is human-made rather than natural. Earth berming or earth sheltering and passive solar heating are ideal combinations.

SUSTAINABLE STRAW BALE HOME

This design calls for straw bale construction, a sustainable building method that uses straw bales (treated with borax to resist insects and rot) covered with wire lath and plaster stucco. The resulting walls are thicker than is usual, and the deep windowsills are perfect for plants and windowseats. For truly local, sustainable building, the straw can be obtained locally, as can the lumber used for the decks.

Features

980 square feet

2 bedrooms

1 full bathroom

Open-concept living space

Fuel-burning stove

Multiple decks

WINDOWS: are set into the deep walls, yielding wide windowsills that work well for plant pots or with window seats

chimney

WALLS: are thicker than in traditional stick construction, due to the size of the straw bales

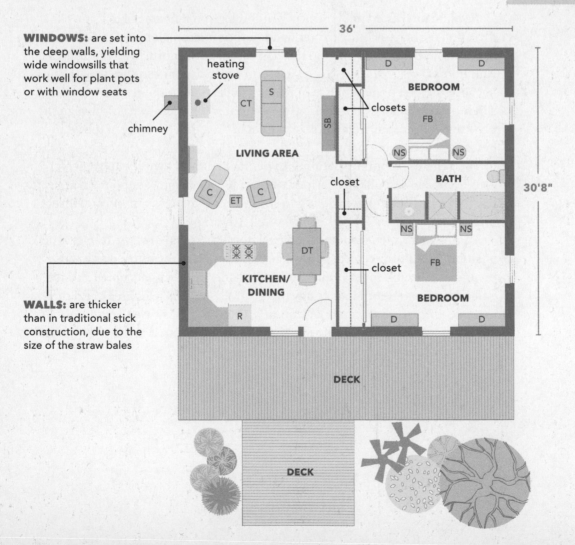

36'

30'8"

heating stove

CT   S

LIVING AREA

C   ET   C

KITCHEN/ DINING

DT

R

D   D

BEDROOM

SB   FB

closets

NS   NS

closet

BATH

NS   NS

closet

FB

BEDROOM

D   D

DECK

DECK

DEEP ROOF OVERHANG: combines with the thick straw bale walls to offer excellent insulative and cooling capacity

STRAW BALE CONSTRUCTION: is a sustainable building method that yields sturdy, well-insulated buildings

TIERED DECKS: can be any shape and size, customized to suit the needs and desires of the homeowners

OFF-THE-GRID EARTH-BERMED HOUSE

This house is earth-bermed on three sides, with the exposed side oriented to the south. With its glass front wall and flagstone patio, it is designed to take advantage of passive solar heating. A woodstove provides cold-weather backup. The structure has a living green roof and a cupola to enhance summer ventilation.

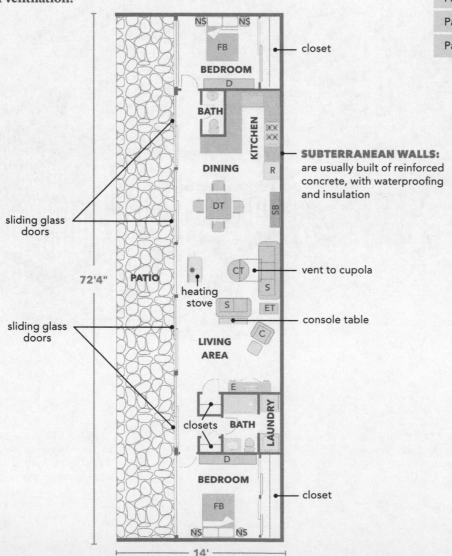

sliding glass doors

sliding glass doors

72'4"

PATIO

14'

NS   NS

FB

BEDROOM

D

closet

BATH

KITCHEN

DINING

R

DT

SB

CT

vent to cupola

S

heating stove

S   ET

console table

C

LIVING AREA

E

closets   BATH   LAUNDRY

D

BEDROOM

FB

NS   NS

closet

SUBTERRANEAN WALLS: are usually built of reinforced concrete, with waterproofing and insulation

CUPOLA: rises from the earthen roof to provide ventilation for the interior living space

MASONRY PATIO: will capture solar heat during the day and slowly release it at night, helping to mediate the interior temperature

EARTHEN BERM: shelters the home on three sides, offering thermal insulation, acting as an air barrier, and minimizing the obtrusiveness of the home in the local environment

OFF-THE-GRID POLE BARN

This house utilizes components and concepts from traditional pole barn design, and it is intended to be energy independent. It is built on a cement slab that houses radiant hot-water heating. It has both solar-electric and solar hot-water collectors, along with a battery array for the solar-electric system housed in a utility room to the rear of the house. It sports a small gas furnace as a backup to the solar hot-water system.

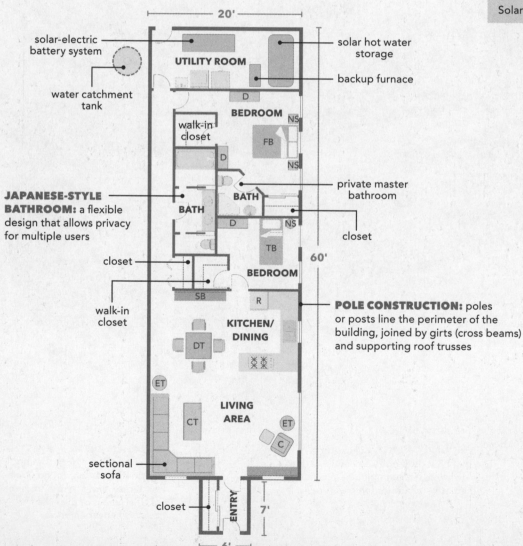

solar-electric battery system

water catchment tank

20'

UTILITY ROOM

solar hot water storage

backup furnace

D

BEDROOM   NS

walk-in closet

FB

D

NS

JAPANESE-STYLE BATHROOM: a flexible design that allows privacy for multiple users

BATH

BATH

private master bathroom

D   NS

closet

TB

closet

walk-in closet

BEDROOM

60'

SB

R

POLE CONSTRUCTION: poles or posts line the perimeter of the building, joined by girts (cross beams) and supporting roof trusses

KITCHEN/ DINING

DT

ET

LIVING AREA

CT

ET

C

sectional sofa

closet

ENTRY   7'

6'

GUTTER: empties rainfall into a water catchment tank; the water can be used for irrigation of the landscaping

SOLAR HOT-WATER COLLECTORS: convert solar power to heat for warming the home's water

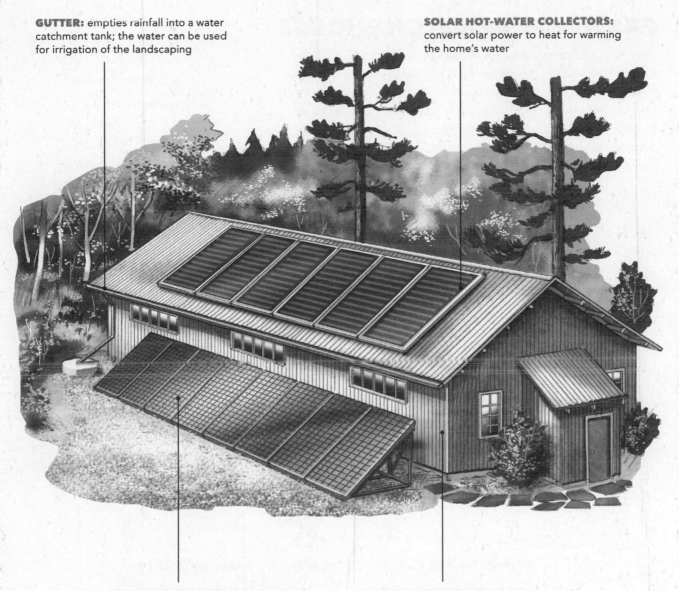

SOLAR-ELECTRIC PANELS: are set in an array to the side of the building, feeding photovoltaic power to a battery storage system housed in the utility room

POLE BUILDING: is simple, economic, and efficient and produces a usually rectangular building with clean lines and a barn-like aesthetic

PASSIVE SOLAR STONE HOUSE

This house is intended to be constructed from local fieldstone. The angled wall of windows should be oriented to the south to take advantage of passive solar heating. The floors are a concrete slab stained a dark color to enhance solar energy absorption. The mass of the stone walls, fireplace, and floor acts as a heat sink, absorbing that solar heat during the day and releasing it at night, as outdoor temperatures cool.

Features

1,248 square feet

2 bedrooms

1 full and 1 three-quarter bathroom

Open-concept living space

Fireplace

Passive solar applications

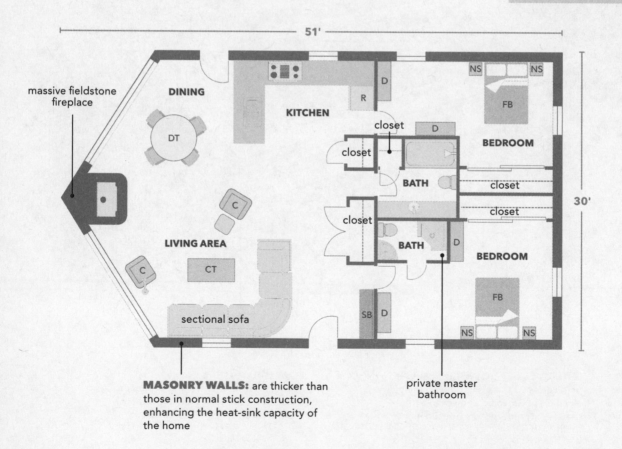

massive fieldstone fireplace

MASONRY WALLS: are thicker than those in normal stick construction, enhancing the heat-sink capacity of the home

private master bathroom

51'

30'

DINING

KITCHEN

DT

closet

closet

closet

BATH

BEDROOM

NS

NS

FB

D

R

D

LIVING AREA

C

C

CT

sectional sofa

closet

BATH

SB

D

D

closet

closet

BEDROOM

FB

NS

NS

HIGH ROOFLINE: creates a one-and-a-half-story interior, with cathedral ceilings throughout

WIDE BANK OF WINDOWS: should be oriented to the south to take advantage of passive solar heating

FIELDSTONE EXTERIOR: works as a heat sink, absorbing heat during the day and releasing it at night, helping to modulate interior temperatures

LOCAL HARVEST LOG HOUSE

This house is designed to be built of local timber; it would be especially eco-friendly if built of timber harvested from the building site. The interior features exposed timbers, and the floors and roof are timber framed. The focus here is on bedroom space; if you didn't need so many bedrooms, you could convert the downstairs bedrooms to additional living space.

Features

1,344 square feet

4 bedrooms

1 full and 2 three-quarter bathrooms

Open-concept living space

Deck

WINDOWS: are set into the deep log walls, yielding wide windowsills that work well for plant pots or with window seats

LOG TIMBERS: make for thick walls

FIRST FLOOR

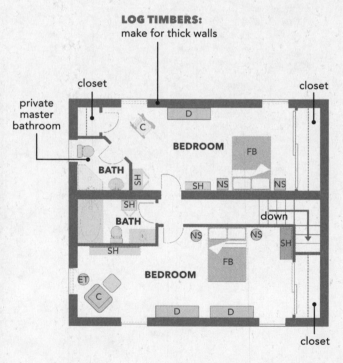

SECOND FLOOR

LOG CONSTRUCTION: is a classic early American architectural style that works well in a wooded or rural setting

NOTCHED LOG-OVER-LOG CORNERS: can be as simple as the Lincoln Log construction of your youth or as dramatic as you can dream, with sweeping flares and staggered curves

FRONT DECK: could easily be replaced with a covered porch, if the homeowners preferred a more sheltered outdoor living space

NATURALLY COOLED WARM-CLIMATE HOUSE

With sliding glass doors on all sides, this house is designed for a warm or tropical climate. The deep roof of the wraparound porch blocks light from shining directly into the first-floor windows, allowing the house to have indirect natural light without solar heating. That deep roof also protects windows and doors from rain, allowing them to be open for ventilation even in inclement weather. The clay tile roof helps reflect sunlight, and its thermal mass absorbs sunlight rather than passing the solar heat into the home, which helps keep the home cool during the day.

Features

1,400 square feet
2 bedrooms
1 full bathroom
Open-concept living space
Fuel-burning stove
Wraparound porch

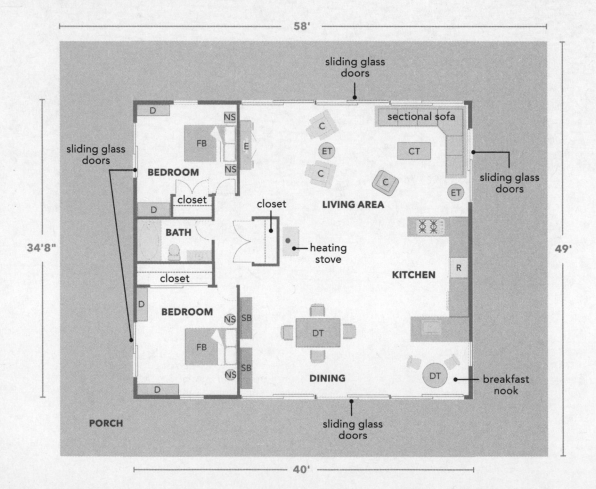

SLIDING GLASS DOORS: line the perimeter of the house, allowing for cross-ventilation from all angles

DEEP WRAPAROUND PORCH: shades the interior from direct sunlight

CEMENT SLAB FLOORING: for both the porch and the interior keeps the house cool underfoot

CHAPTER 4

RETROFITS: FINDING AND RENOVATING A COMPACT HOUSE

NO DISCUSSION OF COMPACT HOUSES WOULD BE COMPLETE WITHOUT A LOOK AT THE WIDE RANGE ALREADY IN EXISTENCE.

Bungalows, Cape Cod cottages, ranch houses, and other types of small homes that predominated housing development in the twentieth century can be found in ready supply across the country. And these houses are ripe for retrofits, with solid bones but infrastructure, appliances, technology, and decor in need of updating.

Renovating a compact house, rather than building a new one, has great appeal for many people of different backgrounds, lifestyles, and incomes. A renovation can be less expensive overall, or at least in the long term, as you can live in a home while you're renovating it. It also allows you to use sweat equity to your advantage. If you're working with a historic home, you may be eligible for special low-cost mortgages, grants, and home-improvement loans to restore the house. And a renovation has a smaller carbon footprint than a new house, simply because it doesn't require as much in the way of new materials.

How we organize and assign interior space in our homes has changed over time to reflect current lifestyles and technologies. Formal living rooms are disappearing in favor of family rooms. Areas that have limited function, such as hallways, are vanishing. Kitchens are larger and offer seating for noncooking guests. Houses have more bathrooms, and master baths are not uncommon. You won't find many of these features in older homes, but there's no reason to assume that they can't have them. When you're thinking about renovating a particular house, you have to think about how the space was *intended* to function, how it *does* function, how you *want* it to function, and *what is possible*, in terms of redesigning the interior spaces to make the home function as you'd like. Design, structure, ergonomics, style, energy efficiency, sustainability, and technology all play a role here.

Good design reflects contemporary ideas. That is, good design is current in its awareness of materials, techniques, technologies, and notions of how we use our living spaces. And while good design is independent of style — it can be neo-Bauhaus, Federalist, midcentury-modern chic, or what have you — it is highly personal and driven by the use patterns of the individual household. Instead of any preconceived ideas of what constitutes a good home today, good design approaches the concept of "home" afresh each time. And that allows you to look at an existing house with fresh eyes and decide for yourself whether it has the potential to be a comfortable, beautiful, easy-to-live-in home for *you*.

ADVANTAGES OF RETROFITTING VERSUS BUILDING NEW

▶ The utilities are already on-site: water, sewer, electric, gas, Internet, cable TV, and so on. This saves both time and money.

▶ Most existing houses have mature landscaping and established lawns. With new construction, you'll need professional landscaping, which can be expensive and takes a long time to come into its own. A good shade tree takes from 20 to 30 years or more to mature to a useful size.

▶ Often you can live in a house while it's being renovated. (For this to work you have to be able to tolerate some degree of construction chaos for an extended period of time.)

▶ Renovating a house is usually less expensive than building a new house, especially if you're at all handy and can do some of the work yourself. The more work you can do yourself (sweat equity), the less it will cost for the same square footage compared with new construction.

▶ If character is your thing, older houses have it. Whether it's the warm patina of age or the discriminating details of a certain period, older houses have earned their character in a way new houses are hard put to match. It's really hard to fake the aging process.

▶ From an environmental standpoint, renovating an existing house makes a lot of sense. It requires less in the way of new materials and allows you to recycle a lot of the existing materials and infrastructure.

RESTORATION VERSUS REMODELING VERSUS REPURPOSING

In just about any real estate market today, you can find housing in a range of styles, square footages, and ages. Of course, they're also in various states of disrepair and outdatedness. But if you're up for a renovation project, you can get a great deal on what can become the home of your dreams. Whatever the type of housing you're looking at, there are three possibilities for renovation: restoration, remodeling, and repurposing.

Restoration

Restoration entails renovation with a sense of historical architectural correctness. The degree of correctness varies depending on the homeowner and community. While there are purists, insisting upon absolute historical correctness can lead to uncomfortable houses. A historically correct 1940s kitchen, for example, simply couldn't meet modern needs. Intelligent restoration celebrates what was good about the past and updates or disregards what was not good. The eclecticism of elements in the marriage of old and new gives the homeowner the best of both worlds.

As a general rule of thumb, restorers keep the exterior of a home historically correct and upgrade interior utilities and appliances to current standards. In particular, they'll focus on remodeling bathrooms and kitchens and, since older homes are notoriously short on storage space, adding more closets and shelving. Depending on how close they want to stick to the historical standard, restorers may consider upgrades as radical as removing walls to open up interior spaces, adding windows to bring more natural light into the home, or putting a swimming pool in the backyard.

Throughout America many towns and cities have designated historical districts, where homes and other buildings are usually all of an equal age and stature. Any renovations in such a district are usually required to adhere to a certain standard of historical correctness, as decided by a historical review board, though the regulations vary in their strictness. Those that lean toward being very strict may dictate the building materials residents can use and even the colors they can paint their exterior trim. Some people think of historical review boards as an infringement on their individual liberties and freedoms; others view them as a guide to correct restoration. However you may feel about the review boards, buying a home in the neighborhoods they supervise can be a profitable investment; homes in historical districts can sell for 10 to 20 percent more than homes just outside those districts.

Many historical districts have established preservation associations that offer help and advice about construction, reconstruction, and zoning within the district and also act as a social group for like-minded homeowners. Some even hold classes dealing with renovation issues of plumbing, carpentry, electrical wiring, and so on.

Remodeling

Remodeling is similar to restoration in some ways but is not encumbered by the constraints of historical correctness. You have far more design freedom in remodeling a house. You can use contemporary materials without the need to disguise them as historically correct materials. You will not be required to have utilities buried underground or enter the home from the rear of the property, as is required in some historical districts, and you'll be free to add solar panels or other outdoor equipment wherever it is most efficient. And you can add on to your home in whatever way you wish, building out porches or decks or adding rooms.

Repurposing

As the name implies, repurposing means redesigning an existing structure for a new purpose. You might, for example, purchase a shop, church, or other commercial space, and repurpose it as a living space. This concept has become especially popular in urban areas, where old factories or office buildings, which generally encompass lots of open space, are often redesigned as loft apartments.

Some repurposing involves converting a space into two or more units, with one devoted to living and the other a storefront, workshop, or studio. This kind of repurposed housing is popular with artists, architects, craftsmen, and tradesmen who want to live near their work area. In an urban area, a repurposed multistory building usually designates the first floor as commercial space and gives over the upper floors to living space. Some such buildings even incorporate roof decks with hot tubs and potted gardens. This arrangement works well. The commercial space is easily accessible at ground level. The living space is above this with the bedrooms on the higher floors, where the air is fresher. This removes the living space from the commotion of the street level. And rooftop gardens create an isolated oasis even in the midst of a city.

Preservation Resources

If you're interested in home restoration and preservation, look up the National Trust for Historic Preservation (NTHP). This organization is dedicated to quality restoration and preservation of America's architectural treasures. It supports not just early colonial architecture but a cross-section of historically important structures from colonial times through current times. The NTHP also supports organizations that endeavor to preserve historical neighborhoods or communities.

BEFORE YOU BEGIN

Before you begin house hunting, make a list of what you want from a house, distinguishing between *needs* and *wants*. Needs are nonnegotiables; for example, you might *need* three bedrooms, more than one bathroom, and a roomy kitchen. Wants are more flexible; you might like to have a master bathroom, or you might prefer to have four bedrooms, so that you can have a separate guest room. But know what you want and need before you start looking at houses. That way you will not get caught up in the excitement of a new and interesting property. Remember that it is the job of a good real estate agent to get you excited about whichever property you're looking at.

If you're planning on doing the renovation work yourself, you'll also want to have some idea of the limits of your skills. Then you can determine the scale of renovation you're interested in and capable of tackling.

If you're planning to take out a loan to purchase the home, you might also consider getting preapproval from a bank for a mortgage. Then you'll know your price range. Keep in mind that you're planning a renovation here, and you need to take into account the cost of the renovation work. You may be able to roll the renovation costs into your mortgage, especially if you're planning on hiring contractors who can give you written estimates; talk to a bank officer about this possibility. Regardless, you'll need to estimate the cost of renovation and add it to the cost of the home before you can ascertain the true and full cost of your home renovation.

HOUSE HUNTING

So you're thinking about buying and renovating a house. This poses an important question: what are the criteria to use when evaluating a house? In a lot of cases, comparing houses is like comparing apples to oranges. This house has a porch, and that one a garage. This one is 1,400 square feet, and that one 900. This one has a nicely landscaped yard; that one has a beautifully updated bathroom; the other one needs a complete rehabilitation of the kitchen, but it's a lot cheaper.

To compare houses at the most basic level, it helps to break down the numbers to common values. Let's examine some of the factors.

Comparing Cost and Value

The first step is to establish the cost and projected value of a property. Start by surveying at least six houses (ten is better) in the same area that are selling within a narrow price range. This seems like a lot of footwork, but after you do it you will have a clearer idea of what you can purchase for your dollar in the area. Remember, all real estate values are local. Always compare properties that are in the same neighborhood or area.

Then chart the houses so you can compare features and how they affect price. Set up a spreadsheet listing the following for each of the properties:

▶ Price

▶ Location

▶ Condition

▶ Number of rooms

▶ Number and condition of bathrooms

▶ Number of bedrooms

▶ Kitchen (eat-in or not?) and condition of appliances

▶ Outbuildings (garage, etc.)

▶ Square footage of living space

▶ Attic

▶ Cellar

▶ Porch, deck, or patio

▶ Size and condition of yard

▶ Benefits/drawbacks of location

▶ Cost per square foot of living space

Now it's time to evaluate the potential value of each property. There are, of course, intangibles — your emotional reaction to the style and setting of the property, the fact that you know (or loathe) the neighbors, and so on. But for the purposes of comparison, it's best to stick with financial factors. These figures will work together with the intangibles to determine your decision. You'll want to know three things:

▶ The projected highest selling price for the home when renovated

▶ The cost to bring the house up to that value

▶ The projected value per square foot of renovated living space

The projected maximum resale value is a parameter for your decision, not an actual limit to your work. It simply tells you the highest value your home can have as a strictly financial asset. And keep in mind that houses *do* have limits to their value, no matter how much work you put into them. For example, if you're surveying houses selling for $150,000 to $200,000 in a certain neighborhood, you'll want to know that even the freshest-looking house in that neighborhood won't sell for more than $275,000. There are exceptions — such as if a successful high-tech firm moves to town, or gold is discovered underfoot — but generally such limits hold true.

The projected renovation cost is similarly a parameter, not a limit. You may decide to do less or more work to any particular house. This figure is simply an objective guideline for the purpose of comparison.

And now it's time for that comparison. Add the projected renovation costs (to bring the house up to its maximum value) to the purchase price for each property. Note that figure alongside the projected maximum value. Then compare the figures for all the properties (you can even convert them to ratios if that's helpful). The results of your comparison should tell you which houses have the most potential value to gain from renovation.

Comparing Sweat Equity Value

If you're planning on doing some of the renovation work yourself, or building sweat equity, you will want to compare the potential sweat equity value for each property. For the sake of this discussion, let's say you've narrowed down your choices to two houses with the same purchase price and are trying to choose between them. House A needs a new kitchen and bathroom, and House B needs a new driveway. Let's say the materials you would need for a new kitchen and bathroom in House A would cost about $8,000 total. Adding labor costs, a contractor might give you an estimate of $16,000 for the work. The old driveway of House B needs to be removed, a new base put down, and then the driveway repaved; a contractor might give you an estimate of $15,000 for the work.

If you plan to use contractors for both projects, House B might be a better choice simply due to the fact that the renovation would cost less. But now let's factor in sweat equity. If you're handy, you could do the kitchen and bath renovation in House A yourself and cut the cost by half. But if you don't own excavation equipment, a dump truck, and a paving machine (and who does?), you probably wouldn't be able to tackle the driveway rehab at House B. Based on these facts, House A seems the better choice.

Comparing Value by Square Footage

Another way to compare houses is to compare the value per square foot at the time of purchase price and at maximum resale value. To calculate these numbers you simply divide first the purchase price and then the maximum resale value by the number of square feet of the house.

You could then calculate the percentage of return per square foot. Let's say you bought a house at $99 per square foot and sold it for $127 per square foot. That is a difference of $28 dollars per square foot. In a 1,000-square-foot house that you purchase for $100,000, that represents a gain of 28 percent. A large property might return more dollars in equity, but a smaller property might return a much higher percentage of equity. So don't be seduced by the idea that bigger is always better. Given that the smaller property would take less time to renovate and requires a smaller initial investment, it could actually be the better investment.

Other Considerations of Value

There are a number of factors to take into consideration that go beyond the basic finances of a house:

▶ **Your timeline.** If your time is unlimited, taking several years to complete a project may not be a problem. Tradesmen choreographed to work in unison can get the job done very quickly. The first way is less expensive and slower; the second, more expensive (but usually quicker).

▶ **Your abilities and skills.** Redoing a house takes a broad array of skills: carpentry, plumbing, electrical, drywall, painting and trim work — not to mention design skills, record keeping, scheduling, some light bookkeeping, and communicating with subcontractors and building supply stores. You do not have to know everything, but you do need to be willing to learn as you go. This might entail making mistakes that will have to be corrected.

▶ **Time available.** If you work 50 to 60 hours a week, you may not have the time to undertake a house redo by yourself. And you may have other commitments on your time (friends, family, kids, etc.) as well. These are important concerns and may determine if the project gets finished or not. You don't want to find that after you have completed the project, no one, not even your kids, is speaking to you.

▶ **Your finances.** A shoestring project needs a lot of your effort. Having a big budget allows you the luxury of watching someone else do the grunt work. There may be a mix of the two approaches that is right for you.

▶ **Your tenaciousness.** Many people with the dream of redoing a house run out of steam before they finish. It's important to schedule in downtime to recharge your batteries. A little downtime is better than burning out.

▶ **Your flexibility and willingness to work.** How long can you live with the disruption and dirt of working on a property? This boils down to enjoyment or the lack thereof. If you find it personally rewarding to work with your hands, your project might be a labor of love. If you hate that kind of work, it could be a painful experience best left to others. I find saving time at the end of each working day to clean up well makes living with construction more tolerable.

▶ **Local building codes and ordinances.** These may change from town to town and affect how you rehab a house. People generally do what they can themselves and hire others to do what they can't. The exception would be where local zoning requirements are involved. Many municipalities require that public gas service, city water service, and electrical breaker panels be installed by licensed tradesmen. Further, many municipalities require that all work done on rental or commercial properties be done by licensed tradesmen.

▶ **Building regulations in historical districts.** Homes in designated historical districts sometimes have stringent parameters guiding any renovation work. You can check in with the local historical review board or municipal building department to find out about such regulations. (And see page 181 for more on historical districts.)

RENOVATION: A CASE STUDY

A few years ago I decided it was time to sell my old house and move on to a new project. I was living in a historical district in the inner city of Allentown, Pennsylvania. I had lived there for more than 20 years, and over that time I had, as a contractor, built a number of summer cabins and houses and refurbished a number of older houses, from colonial fieldstone farmhouses to gingerbread Victorians to contemporary condos.

The challenge was, what would I do now? I had always been interested in redoing a 1950s-era house (usually described as midcentury modern) and decided this might be a good time for it.

Finding a House

I started by making a wish list of the features I would like in this house:

▶ **Small.** I was living in 1,400 square feet at the time, but as an empty nester, smaller seemed better. I thought something in the range of 1,000 square feet would do it.

▶ **Two bedrooms plus an office.** I wanted a master bedroom, a guest bedroom, and a home office. Though there are various ways to fit a home office into small spaces, this probably meant that I was looking for a three-bedroom home.

▶ **One floor.** This is an idea I would not have considered ten years ago, but now that I was an aging pre–baby boomer, it seemed a legitimate concern.

▶ **Good bones.** I was looking for a house that had "good bones" — that is, it was structurally sound — but needed a total cosmetic redo and updating. It takes a little practice to look beyond the cosmetic to the structure underneath, but it's important. Without major demolition and rebuilding, a house with "bad bones" can never be brought up to the standard of one with a good basic structure.

▶ **Three-car garage.** I was looking for a three-car garage: two for cars and one for my travel trailer and camping gear. When I began my search this seemed like an absurd possibility. Small midcentury houses have, at best, a one-car garage. (But I got lucky.)

▶ **Small yard.** I wanted a yard, but not a large one. The idea of spending a lot of time cutting grass doesn't appeal to me — been there, done that. I also wanted a space for a garden. Around a half acre seemed ideal for my needs.

That Old House Character

It is sometimes impossible to duplicate the details and materials found in older houses. I once owned a bungalow-style house that used chestnut trim throughout, on window and door trim, baseboards, the paneling in the dining room, and the wainscoting in the kitchen. The straight-grained chestnut wood had aged over the years to a rich, dark color that imparted a warm, homey feel to the house. I loved it. I would wholeheartedly recommend chestnut trim in just about any house. But since the blight of the early part of the last century, chestnut wood has not been available. Unless you buy it from a salvage yard (and it's rare to find it there), the only way to get that chestnut character in a house is to buy a period house. Staining new woodwork simply does not yield the natural depth of character that real chestnut does over time.

▶ **Good resale value.** I wanted a house that would maintain its value. I know that a small house, in good condition, will always have appeal as a starter house. A young couple just starting out will naturally mature into several kids, and that's when good schools become an issue. So, though I don't myself have kids at home, I narrowed my search region to one of the best school districts in my area.

▶ **Fixer-upper.** Choosing a small house that needed work would allow me to buy without a mortgage. With no mortgage, and fixing it up out of pocket, I would have a good degree of financial flexibility.

I looked for a little more than three months. I finally found a small ranch house, just under 1,000 square feet. It was built in 1949, had been purchased by its current owner in the mid-1960s, and was in dire need of work. It sat on a half-acre-plus lot with some nice mature shade trees and room for a garden plot. There was a back porch and a three-car garage. One bay of the garage had a 12-foot-high door and could house a 30-foot trailer; another bay had an auto-service pit and a furnace and could be heated whenever necessary. Inside the house, the bathroom had not been updated since the house was built and had serious rot issues around the tub. The kitchen had been redone in the 1960s and showed it. The interior of the house was covered with dark, cheap, early-1960s plastic-coated paneling. The floors were covered with orange wall-to-wall carpeting with lots of stains. But under the carpeting I found red oak flooring. The carpet pads had fused to the floor finish, but I knew that any residue could be sanded off fairly easily and the floors would refinish beautifully. The windows were original and leaked cold air badly; they'd have to be replaced with something more efficient.

The foundation was poured concrete, with a large I beam running the length of the house. There was no cracking in the foundation and no evidence of flooding in the cellar. The heating system was an oil-fired hot-water baseboard system, about 15 years old. The house had large eave overhangs that would shade the interior in the summer while allowing the sun in during the winter. The water was public, the sewage private (though I'm told public sewage is on its way). The septic system and drain field (which was all but plugged with solids) dated from the original construction of the house and would need to be replaced.

Making a Renovation Plan

When I first saw the home, I had been assured that a lot of demolition work would be necessary to repair the walls and structure. I measured the house carefully and began to redesign it on paper. I would carry pencil and sketchbook around with me and make notes whenever ideas struck me. But you never know what you'll find when you begin a renovation project, and I got lucky. When I removed the old paneling, I found underneath it thick (five-eighths-inch) drywall with a finish coat of plaster, all intact. There were virtually no cracks in any of the walls. They were in great shape.

The demolition process provided an insight into the quality the original builder had put into the house. In the postwar 1950s, new housing generally was built fast and cheap to meet the demands of a vigorous market and the limited funds of young families. Many new houses in that era were purchased through the GI Bill, with no money down and very reasonable interest rates. Many builders sacrificed quality to produce the largest houses for the dollar. But the builder of this house was producing quality construction when it was not the popular trend.

I decided to rethink the reconstruction with an eye to keeping as much of the original interior as was practical. I wanted to make a point of respecting the quality work of the original builder, while obliterating all the bad remodeling that had been done in the late 1960s. My new plan was to maximize the living space without changing the footprint of the house. I had four primary goals:

- ▶ **Open up the interior.** This home was a typical 1950s ranch: a number of small rooms interconnected with doors. I wanted to open the space up and make it more accessible.

- ▶ **Add closet space.** Like most houses built in this era, the house seriously lacked closet space.

- ▶ **Demolish the bathroom and rebuild it from the studs out.** This was probably the worst room of the house. A half century of mold and rot had destroyed it.

- ▶ **Redesign and rebuild the kitchen.** The kitchen was essentially a Pullman layout: long and narrow with a central walkway. I liked the layout, but the fixtures and appliances represented the worst of past remodeling. I planned to rip out most of it and install new floor and wall tile, cabinetry, appliances, plumbing, insulation, wiring, and so on.

Converting Cellars to Living Space

One common way to increase the living space in a compact home is by repurposing the cellar. A modern finished cellar can house an in-law apartment, a family/game room, a studio or workshop, or what have you. Whatever the choice, you'll likely want to install a bathroom.

In the past, one common problem with cellar bathrooms was getting the wastewater into the sewer system. Thankfully, great advances have been made in "flush-up" systems. Modern flush-up systems consist of a small plastic chamber installed below the cellar floor that contains a pump and operating system that pump bathroom waste into the sewer system. These systems are equipped with ventilation equipment, so no smells enter the living space. Many also function as sump pumps; they are fitted with a valve that allows any groundwater that rises up or seeps into the cellar to drain into the unit and be pumped into the sewer system.

With the demolition and rebuilding work greatly reduced from what I had expected, I had extra funds, which I directed toward extending the living space by enclosing the porch and finishing the cellar.

The southeast-facing porch ran the length of the house. I decided to enclose the space and convert it to a sunroom, adding insulation, baseboard heating, Berber carpeting, energy-efficient windows, a combination wood-and-coal-burning stove, and a powder room with a toilet and sink. The extra heat from the stove and the solar gain from the windows can be directed into the house to supplement the winter heating. It has since become my favorite space in the house. I start my day there each morning with coffee and end it there by the fire on cold winter nights.

The cellar was a blank slate, housing only the furnace, fuel oil tank, and laundry sink at one end and an unused pump room at the other. The bulk of my uncommitted funds would go here. My plans for this space included the following:

▶ A family room with a wet bar with a sink, small refrigerator, microwave, and two-burner induction cooktop; a woodstove and baseboard heat; and Berber carpeting; along with a full bathroom with a large spa tub and a two-person sauna

▶ General storage space

▶ A pantry for the storage of canned goods

▶ A washer and dryer near the laundry sink

▶ An area devoted to a fly-tying bench (I love to fly-fish)

▶ A combination wine cellar and root cellar in the former pump room (a cast-concrete-walled room that was completely underground)

The original house had 912 square feet of living space. With my renovations, I added 708 square feet of living space in the cellar. The sunporch added another 323 square feet. With these modifications, 912 square feet became 1,943 square feet without expanding beyond the existing footprint of the house.

On the following pages you'll find "before" and "after" floor plans for the little ranch house. Following them are "before" and "after" plans for some other compact houses I've renovated.

ORIGINAL FLOOR PLAN

The ranch home was structurally sound but sorely in need of stylistic, mechanical, and functional updates. The kitchen was outdated and inefficient, while the bathroom had lost the battle against rot and mold. Closet space was inadequate, and the unfinished basement had long been neglected.

MAIN FLOOR

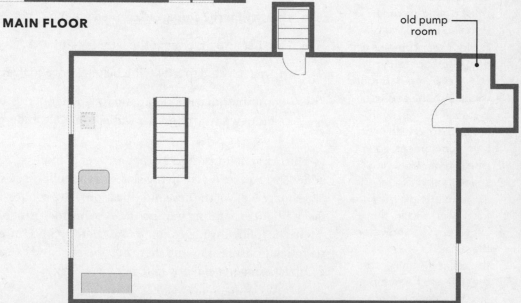

CELLAR

FINAL FLOOR PLAN

By enclosing the porch, adding a deck, and finishing the basement, the renovation more than doubled the living space in the house, turning it into a spacious, comfortable home with an easy transition from indoors to out.

The bathroom, gutted and rebuilt, occupies the same space but is now modernized and functional, and it has been joined by another full bathroom in the basement (making that space excellent guest quarters) and a half bathroom on the sunporch (for cleaning up after gardening, fishing, and other grubby endeavors).

The kitchen, slightly redesigned, is up-to-date and easy to use, and it now features an eat-in table. A home office is tucked into the basement, along with a wet bar and wine/root cellar.

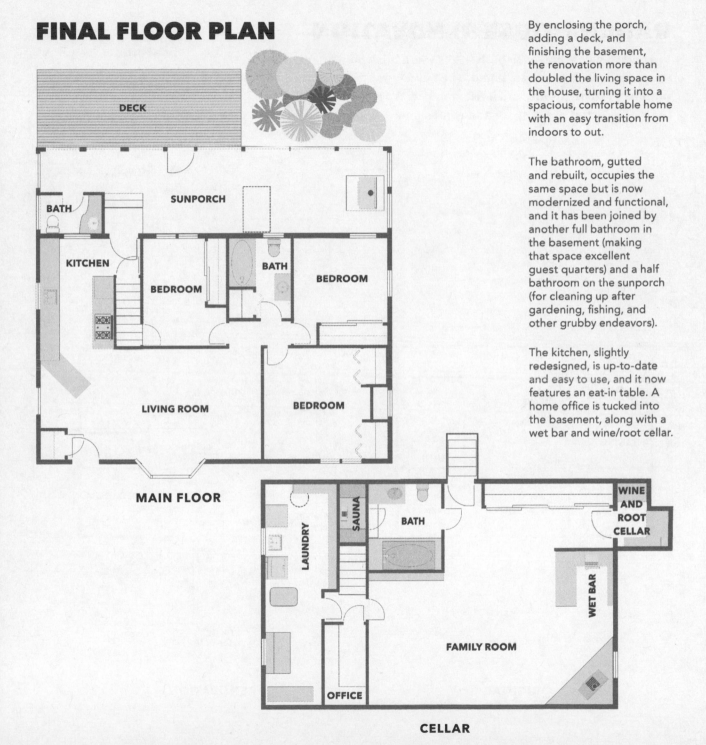

DECK

BATH

SUNPORCH

KITCHEN

BEDROOM

BATH

BEDROOM

LIVING ROOM

BEDROOM

MAIN FLOOR

LAUNDRY

SAUNA

BATH

WINE AND ROOT CELLAR

WET BAR

FAMILY ROOM

OFFICE

CELLAR

RANCH HOUSE RENOVATION

This ranch house had been built in 1933. As a brick house it was structurally strong but very dated. The interior was divided into a number of small rooms, and it felt cramped. We renovated the home to reflect a better use of space and contemporary housing needs.

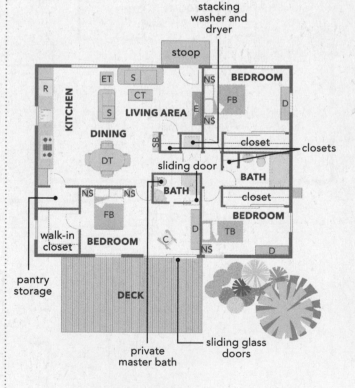

Features

1,066 square feet

3 bedrooms

1 full and 1 three-quarter bathroom

Open-concept living space

Deck

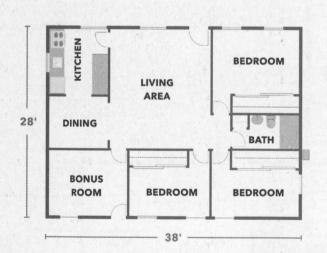

ORIGINAL

RENOVATION

MASTER BEDROOM: now has not only its own bathroom but its own deck, with sliding glass doors providing lots of natural light

TRADITIONAL RANCH SHAPE: Is maintained, but the inside of the home is now opened up, with an open-concept living space, expanded kitchen, and additional closet space

VICTORIAN RENOVATION

This gingerbread Victorian home, built in 1896, was very dated, with both the kitchen and bathroom inadequate by modern standards. The project was a complete redo: the wiring, plumbing, and heating replaced, kitchen and bathroom gutted, new roof installed, floors refinished, clapboards replaced, and painting inside and out. When we were done, the homeowners had the house painted as a classic five-color Victorian.

Features
1,176 square feet
2 bedrooms
2 three-quarter and 1 half bathrooms
Patio
Porch

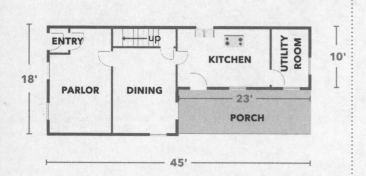

FIRST FLOOR

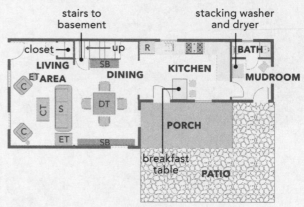

FIRST FLOOR

SECOND FLOOR

ORIGINAL

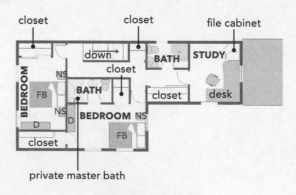

SECOND FLOOR

RENOVATION

CLASSIC VICTORIAN DETAILS:
include a slate roof, shingle and
clapboard siding, and decorative arches
over the doorways and windows

MASTER BEDROOM:
has taken over the space
previously dedicated to the
hall and bath, and it now
features a private bathroom
and ample closet storage

PRIVATE REAR PORCH: is
now joined by an expansive
patio, opening up the outdoor
living space

ROW HOUSE RENOVATION

This brick row house, on a small city lot, was a condemned property, with 23 code violations filed against it, that the homeowners purchased for one dollar. It was a top-to-bottom redo, including wiring, plumbing, heating, kitchen, bath, flooring, walls, roof, and siding.

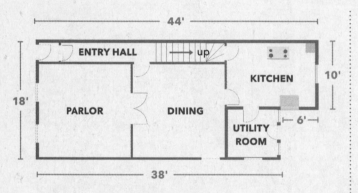

FIRST FLOOR

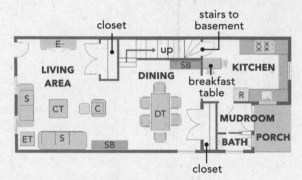

FIRST FLOOR

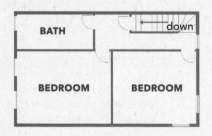

SECOND FLOOR

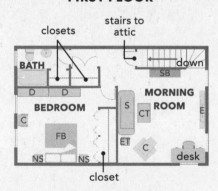

SECOND FLOOR

ORIGINAL

RENOVATION

FEDERAL-ERA ROW HOUSE DETAILS: include a simple silhouette, brick exterior, and stone lintels

MORNING ROOM: now occupies the back half of the second story, a private and quiet spot for relaxing

FARMHOUSE RENOVATION

This frame farmhouse was built in the 1880s and was in dire disrepair. The plaster walls were in bad shape and had to be torn down; new drywall was hung. We replaced the entire plumbing and heating systems to bring them up to modern standards. And we designed a new addition with a country kitchen on the first floor and a master bedroom suite on the second floor.

Features
1,400 square feet
4 bedrooms
2 full and 1 three-quarter bathrooms
Woodstove
Solar hot water

FIRST FLOOR

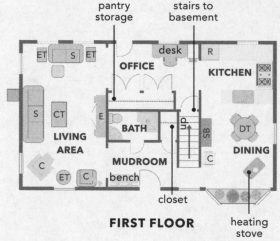

FIRST FLOOR

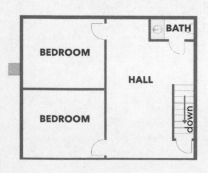

SECOND FLOOR

ORIGINAL

SECOND FLOOR

RENOVATION

NEW ADDITION: is seamlessly integrated with the existing house by virtue of the new roof and replica clapboard siding

FIRST-FLOOR LIVING AREA: has expanded across the width of the house, making it a large, comfortable, inviting space

BOW WINDOW: in the new addition floods the dining room and kitchen with natural light

ALPHABETICAL LISTING OF PLANS

INDEX

Page numbers in *italics* indicate illustrations.

ALSO BY GERALD ROWAN

COMPACT CABINS
Simple living in 1,000 square feet or less — includes
62 design interpretations for every taste.
216 pages. Paper. ISBN 978-1-60342-462-2.

OTHER STOREY TITLES YOU WILL ENJOY

DREAM COTTAGES
by Catherine Tredway
Twenty-five illustrated plans for a variety of cottages
designed to meet a wide range of needs and lifestyles.
176 pages. Paper. ISBN 978-1-58017-372-8.

HOME PLAN DOCTOR
by Larry W. Garnett
The essential companion to buying home plans,
from understanding basic design principles
to requesting needed modifications.
224 pages. Paper. ISBN 978-1-58017-698-9.

HOMEOWNER'S ENERGY HANDBOOK
by Paul Scheckel
Practical advice for getting off the grid, plus step-by-step
guides to building green equipment, such as a bicycle-
powered generator, a smokeless camp stove, and more.
288 pages. Paper. ISBN 978-1-61212-016-4.

THE MODULAR HOME
by Andrew Gianino
A comprehensive handbook for prospective buyers
and builders of modular homes and additions.
336 pages. Paper. ISBN 978-1-58017-526-5.

PLYDESIGN
by Philip Schmidt
Distinctive plywood projects for
every room in the house.
320 pages. Paper. ISBN 978-1-60342-725-8.

RUSTIC RETREATS
by David and Jeanie Stiles
Illustrated, step-by-step instructions for more than
20 low-cost, sturdy, beautiful outdoor structures.
160 pages. Paper. ISBN 978-1-58017-035-2.